W9-CQD-480

AMERICAN FARMS
EXPLORING THEIR HISTORY

Exploring Community
History Series Editors

David E. Kyvig
Myron A. Marty

American Farms
Exploring Their
History

R. Douglas Hurt

KRIEGER PUBLISHING COMPANY
MALABAR, FLORIDA
1996

Original Edition   1996

Printed and Published by
KRIEGER PUBLISHING COMPANY
KRIEGER DRIVE
MALABAR, FLORIDA 32950

FROM A DECLARATION OF PRINCIPLES JOINTLY ADOPTED BY A COMMITTEE
OF THE AMERICAN BAR ASSOCIATION AND A COMMITTEE OF PUBLISHERS:
This publication is designed to provide accurate and authoritative information in regard to the subject matter covered. It is sold with the understanding that the publisher
is not engaged in rendering legal, accounting, or other professional service. If legal
advice or other expert assistance is required, the services of a competent professional
person should be sought.

Library of Congress Cataloging-in-Publication Data

Hurt, R. Douglas.
    American farms : exploring their history / R. Douglas Hurt. —
Original ed.
       p.   cm. — (Exploring community history series)
    Includes bibliographical references (p.   ) and index.
    ISBN 0-89464-891-8 (hardcover : alk. paper)
    1. Agriculture—United States—Historiography. 2. Agriculture—
United States—History—Methodology. I. Title. II. Series.
S441.H919   1996
630'.973—dc20   96-11222
                                                                        CIP

10   9   8   7   6   5   4   3   2

FOR
MARY ELLEN, ADLAI, and AUSTIN

CONTENTS

EDITORS' INTRODUCTION

A sense of connection to a community of shared place, circumstance, or interest is an essential of personal well-being. Not to be attached to some community is to be isolated and adrift without either identity or security. Membership in a community offers an individual a sense of what is required of him or her, how to cope with situations confronted, and what to expect in the way of protection or punishment by conforming to or deviating from the norm. Community, in other words, makes it possible for humans to find their way in a chaotic and confusing world.

Communities exist in endless variety and contain a myriad of components. The traditional and most common image of community is the homogeneous village or town, but in modern mass society a community might be a compact, interactive neighborhood, an ethnic/religious affinity, or a professional group brought together by interest rather than geography, or a heterogeneous urban population sharing loyalties and experiences rather than direct personal contact. Today not only residents of Winesburg, Ohio, but those of East Harlem consider themselves a community, as do American and Canadian Ukrainians, Mormons, vegetarians, and dentists spread across the continent. Otherwise unconnected residents of Northeast Ohio unite as a community of sufferers for their professional sports teams just as Des Moines dwellers form a community of 1993 flood veterans. Whatever the nature and strength of the community, it is likely to contain or at least encounter a variety of institutions that carry out political, economic, social, educational, religious, cultural, or other functions that facilitate community life.

Communities are not instantaneous creations but the products of an evolutionary process. To appreciate the nature of a community, not to mention to function successfully in relation to it, requires an understanding of its development over time. Each community, given its distinctive identity, setting, and unfolding circumstances, possesses a unique past. Thus the task of recovering a community's history differs in every case. The discovery and analysis of an individual community's history can provide rewards to long-time members, newcomers, and outsiders alike, but will pose challenges to all.

Communities ought to know, and most instinctively do, that their own particular history is important to them. Recalling nothing of that past puts them in the same position as people suffering from amnesia, unable to remember their origins, their response to needs or challenges, their means of achieving success or dealing with setbacks, their sources of support or opposition, and their goals. History serves society much as memory serves an individual. In imperfect, sometimes distorted, but most often helpful fashion both help identify familiar elements in new situations and provide a guide to appropriate behavior. History also offers a standard of comparison across stretches of time and circumstance that exceed the span of an individual life. In this sense, history is far more than a remembrance of things past. History represents a means of coming to terms with the present, developing an awareness of previous influences, the continuities and distinctiveness in current conditions, and the range of future possibilities. Just as memory helps the individual avoid having to repeat the same discoveries, behaviors, and mistakes, historical knowledge helps a community, as well as any group or individual within it, avoid starting at the beginning each time an issue needs to be addressed.

Even if there is obvious value to a community in understanding its own history, the means of acquiring such self-knowledge are usually less evident, especially when the subject of interest is previously unexamined. Knowledge of the past is commonly gained from books, teachers, museums, films, or other presentations. What is one to do if the subject has never been explored, if there is no book on the topic in the library, if there is no expert to whom to turn? What is to be done in the even more likely circumstance that answers obtained from such sources are insufficient or unsatisfying?

A number of years ago, we began to appreciate that many people would like to explore the past of their own families and communities. Only the lack of research knowledge and confidence stood in their way. We realized from working with undergraduate students, local historical and genealogical societies, and out-of-school adults that any literate person motivated to explore some question regarding the past of his or her immediate surroundings could master most historical research methods, pursue most research possibilities, critically evaluate most potential explanations, and achieve a considerable measure of understanding. We felt it important to empower people to function as historians themselves or evaluate what other historians might say and write about a personally important past.

We began our effort to identify questions of historical significance and interest as well as explain how to investigate them in *Your Family History: A Handbook for Research and Writing* (Arlington Heights, Ill.: Harlan Davidson, 1978). Four years later we continued the undertaking with a larger book, one more widely focused on communities. *Nearby History: Exploring the Past around You* (Nashville: American Association for State and Local History, 1982) was, nevertheless, merely a general overview to a broad and complex subject. The warm reception which greeted *Your Family History* and *Nearby History* encouraged us to carry our notion further by providing specific advice on exploring particular topics. Enlisting historians who were experts on schools, homes, public places, places of worship, and businesses, we edited a five-volume nearby history series published by the American Association for State and Local History. We are now pleased to be able to expand the scope of these efforts through a series of books devoted to exploring community history produced by the Krieger Publishing Company, the first of which was Ann Durkin Keating's *Invisible Networks: Exploring the History of Local Utilities and Public Works.*

No feature on the American landscape has a longer or richer history, and few have greater importance than the farm. From the first European settlements along the New England and Chesapeake shores through plantations of the slave South and the pioneer family farms of the Midwest and Great Plains to the vast commercial fruit-, nut-, and vegetable-growing enterprises of the contemporary Far West, farms have played a vital role in American life. And while to a certain extent, farm life has been isolated and self-sufficient, for the most part farms have been economically, socially, politically, and culturally linked to nearby towns, not to mention the nation as a whole. Farms have been, in other words, an integral part of larger communities. No consideration of American communities would be comprehensive without examining nearby farms, just as no assessment of a farm would be complete without appraising its links to surrounding communities.

R. Douglas Hurt's *American Farms: Exploring Their History* is the first book ever specifically devoted to guiding historical investigation of individual farms. It offers a rich variety of questions to be explored, resources to be exploited, and methods to be employed. In this innovative guide, Doug Hurt draws on his own remarkable background in the history of American agriculture. The author of highly readable, widely admired books and articles on American agricultural history, curator of museum exhibits seen by visitors to the state historical societies of Ohio and Missouri, director of graduate studies in agricultural history at Iowa State University, and editor of the premier journal in the field, *Agricultural History*, he has developed a keen awareness of the needs and interests of those who approach the history of a farm with curiosity but no previous research experience as well as those who bring a scholar's skills but no agricultural background. He has also acquired an admirable capacity to speak clearly and appropriately to both of these audiences. Doug Hurt's *American Farms: Exploring Their History* should have great value for inquiry into the history of a farm, and it should make a major contribution to realizing the goals of the *Exploring Community History* series.

DAVID E. KYVIG, Editor
MYRON A. MARTY, Consulting Editor

PREFACE

This book is intended to aid anyone with an interest in researching and writing the history of a farm. It seeks to aid those who are primarily concerned with a single farm as well as those who wish to begin exploring the broader patterns of North American agriculture by looking at a particular example. It seeks to assist both students and out-of-school independent investigators of the past. As such, it is a how-to-do-it book for farm historians in the United States. It will help the farm historian begin a research project, and it suggests the sources of information and methods that will lead to writing the best possible history. No one will use every approach proposed in this study, but by pursuing many of the sources and techniques, and by using the methods suggested, the farm historian will be well on the way to crafting a useful history that goes beyond isolated facts and nostalgic recollection to produce a meaningful explanation of the farm within the broader context of American agricultural history.

I am grateful for the help of Donald Hutslar, Steve Gordan, and Judith Runestad, who provided several photographs. Bob Harvey and Leo Landis helped with the bibliography, and Homer E. Socolofsky aided the structure. Douglas McManis generously granted permission to use an illustration published in the *Geographical Review*, and Michael Regoli allowed me to draw upon my essay entitled "The Historiography of American Agriculture," published in the *Magazine of History* 5 (Winter 1991): 13–17, for the bibliographical essay. I am also appreciative of the aid given by my research assistants Stephanie Carpenter, Claire Strom, and Kirk Hutson as well as the help of the staff at the State Historical Society of Iowa.

Chapter 1

BREAKING GROUND

The farms in the United States affect the lives of all residents in the nation every day. If anyone is to understand American social, political, and economic history in a comprehensive fashion, they must know about the history of farming. Most people are not farmers or rural residents, and they are several generations removed from farm life. Still, many Americans have an interest in the history of what once was the family farm, even though it might have passed to the ownership of someone else, or they have an interest in the history of a nearby farm that belongs to a friend, relative, or neighbor.

From the colonial period until the late nineteenth century most Americans lived on farms or in towns where the countryside remained only a short walk away, and they may have worked on a farm. They were closely tied to the land. The climate and geography, that is, the environment, shaped the manner in which they farmed, the crops and livestock raised, and their markets. The changing seasons and geographical location of the farm determined their daily tasks. Many farm families planted tobacco and gardens and sheared their sheep in the spring. They harvested wheat and canned vegetables and cooked for harvest hands in the summer. During the autumn, they picked corn and cotton and plowed the fields. In the winter, they broke hemp, slaughtered hogs, and cleared land. Indeed, the farm year was busy for men, women, and children.

Today, fewer people than ever before are farmers. At some time between 1870 and 1880, farmers represented less than 50 percent of the population. Americans, however, remained rural until 1920, when the Bureau of the Census first noted that more than half of the population lived in towns and cities with more than 2,500 people. For the first time in American history the nation had become urban. Thereafter rural daily life began to fade from most memories. Still, farm and rural life continued to play an instrumental role in shaping the American

1

character and economy as it had throughout American history. Even today, when less than 2 percent of the public is engaged in agriculture and only 4.5 million people live on 2.1 million farms, down from 41.9 percent of the population or 29.8 million people on 5.7 million farms at the turn of the twentieth century, agriculture remains fundamental to American life. Indeed, we depend on agriculture for life itself. Today, each farmer produces food and fiber for approximately 100 people. Compared to other countries, the American farmer provides consumers with more food at a lower price than any other free market economy in the world. Other nations depend on American farmers for grain, meat, and fiber. Collectively, American farmers have played a crucial role in the development of the national economy and international trade.

Certainly, the story of American agriculture is fundamental to American national history, but it also has played a major role in shaping state and local history. Moreover, farmers and their families have not only preserved and perpetuated a worldview that agriculture is the rock upon which democracy rests, but more accurately and more importantly they have been innovators, experimenters, and risk-takers in their agricultural endeavors, such as claiming and clearing land, adopting advanced technology, applying new scientific knowledge, and using government to improve their economic standard of living. By so doing, their lives and work have become inextricably linked to scientists, educators, inventors, manufacturers, politicians, bankers, merchants, and environmentalists, among others. Indeed, the history of American agriculture in general and individual farms in particular is both broad and complex, and without the family farm that story would be far different from what it is today.

American agriculture began with family farms. To know the history of any long-standing farm is to know a considerable amount about the American past. No one, for example, can study cotton farming in the pre-Civil War South without reflecting on the nature of slavery and its role in American history; no one can study the effects of the Dust Bowl without learning much about the New Deal and the agricultural programs of Franklin Delano Roosevelt's administration; and no one can study the current activities of a family farm without knowing something about environmental concerns, such as soil erosion, chemical pollution, depletion of water supply, economics, and international trade. To study the history of the family farm is to study the history of American agriculture as well as immigration, westward expansion, railroad building, and other subjects, that is, the nation itself.

It is not enough, however, to know when a farm was founded, the date of purchase of the first reaper, the factors influencing the hiring of migrant labor, or the effects of low prices and high interest rates on farm foreclosures. Farm historians, of course, must learn these things but they will not have exhausted the potential of their topic unless they do more. Investigators will gain far more if they determine what their research means. This requires both interpretation and an understanding of state and national history. Why, for example, were New England farms so different in size from Chesapeake or midwestern farms? The answer lies in settlement patterns determined by religion, economics, and politics. Or, why did hemp farmers in antebellum Kentucky and Missouri stubbornly raise dew-rotted rather than water-rotted hemp even though the latter brought a significantly higher price? To answer that question the historian is led to investigate both American naval policy and czarist Russia. Similarly, the reliance of sharecroppers on cotton during the late nineteenth century necessitates an understanding of national finance, labor resources, reconstruction after the Civil War, and international marketing. To understand the shift from wheat production to dairying in New York at the turn of the twentieth century requires knowledge about the history of railroads, urbanization, and farm technology. Moreover, to understand the importance of a mechanical tomato picker to a corporate farm in California during the late twentieth century calls for knowing about technological change, governmental policy, and international relations.

Simply put, nearby or local history both shapes and is influenced by national and international events. The thorough historian must put the relatively small pieces of a farm's historical puzzle into a larger mosaic. This task requires the consideration of cause and effect as well as the determination of the significance of a farm's developments throughout its history. Only then will the researcher be able to understand the history of the farm in the broadest and most significant way—economically, socially, and politically. Only then will the farm historian be able to answer fully the most difficult and fundamental historical question: How have things come to be as they are?

Agricultural history is an exciting field of inquiry. It can involve the study of great plantations, such as Mount Vernon, or the agricultural elite, such as Thomas Jefferson. Or, it can be the study of small-scale farms operated by owners or tenants. It also includes the study of large-scale ranches, such as the XIT in Texas, and small-scale stock farms in Kansas, corn and hog farms in Iowa, wheat farms in North

Dakota, and peanut farms in Georgia. And, it can cover the study of large corporate farms in California.

Agricultural history can provide insight on the political experience of farmers in movements and organizations, such as Shays's Rebellion, the People's party, or the American Farm Bureau Federation. It can help us understand the daily experience of the men, women, and children, North and South as well as East or West, who earned their living by farming. The history of American farms, then, can involve the study of elites or common men and women at any time or place. Invariably, however, the study of agricultural history begins at the local level, that is, the family farm, ranch, plantation, or corporate enterprise. From there it branches out to include the study of communities, marketing, transportation, science, technology, politics, international affairs, and organizations.The history of a farm, then, presents opportunities for both broad and intensive study of wide-ranging but interrelated subjects, such as land policy, technological and scientific change, education, economics, social and political organizations, and government policy. At first many of these considerations may seem far removed from the history of an individual farm. On close study, however, the historian will find that each is inextricably linked to the farm.

Despite the importance of farming and agricultural history as well as the major contributions historians have already made to scholarship, much historical research, writing, and publication still needs to be accomplished. This work ought to begin at the local level. Economic, political, and diplomatic policy may not seem related to daily life, but public policy, ultimately is determined by the people. What better place to begin the study of American agricultural history in its broadest context than with the history of a farm. The researcher, of course, does not need to live on or have a personal link to a farm to study it. Rather, the historian only needs an interest in the farm, a particular family, the local community, or agricultural history. The history of the farm is as close as the collections in the nearest library, archives, or historical society. If the historian does not live on or close to the farm, however, a trip to see it and to visit with the owners or operators will be highly useful at some point during the research process.

No matter the nature of the farm to be studied—family or corporate enterprise (whether 100 or 100,000 acres)—the historian will benefit from a clear plan, that is, a research agenda. Such a plan may evolve as research proceeds and more is learned, but it is far preferred to chaotic, disorganized inquiry. That research goal would be based on purpose and design, and it ought to be based on solid, incisive questions. Simply put, the historian first needs to determine what is to be done, and then decide how to do it. A set of questions will help the farm historian maintain focus and control of the research project as well as strengthen and hone the narrative. During the course of one's research, other questions frequently will arise, based on the sources being consulted. The historian will want to deal with those questions and go wherever the evidence leads. Although the historian can and often should work with a thesis, a central theme, or explanation in mind, he or she must guard against the dangers of rigid theory which at the worst translates into ideology. History based on ideology often reduces to fiction, because it forces the historian to forego objectivity and shape evidence to meet preconceived conclusions. In contrast, an approach based on answering a set of questions will help keep the historian focused on the possible alternative realities of the past.

The following topics and questions can be used as a place to start. The farm historian should be flexible in order to accept those that are appropriate while rejecting those that are not suitable for a particular research project.

Land Acquisition

Who first claimed the land?
When was it claimed?
Did the family or first owner purchase the land from the government or speculators?
What were the original boundaries of the farm?
How have those boundaries changed over time?
Why did the boundaries change?
Where are the boundaries today?

Land Use

What crops were originally raised on the farm?
Why were those crops raised and not others?
What livestock were originally raised?
Why did the early owners or tenants raise that livestock instead of other kinds, for example, hogs instead of cattle or sheep?
What changes in cropping patterns have been made in the history of the farm, such as changes from wheat to corn, sorghum to sugar beets, tobacco to cotton, or small grains to dairying?
What changes have been made in livestock, such as a switch from dairy cattle to sheep or Angus to Santa Gertrudis beef cattle?

How has the look of the farm changed over the years, such as trees cleared, marshes drained, or land leveled for irrigation?

Daily Life

How has daily life changed? Were there notable turning points or just recognizable differences at 50-year intervals?

What was expected of the women who lived on this farm from generation to generation?

How did women meet their obligations?

What were the responsibilities of the men?

How did men fulfill their duties?

What was expected of the children?

How did the children meet these requirements?

How did the responsibilities of men, women, and children change with the seasons?

How has transportation between the farm and the nearby towns changed?

What were the daily routines of the farm family from the earlier generations to the most recent?

How did these daily activities alter with the seasons?

How did technological change affect the farm home, that is, when did the farm get electricity, and from what source?

When did it get radio, television, telephone, refrigeration, washing machines, vacuum cleaners, and electric or gas stoves?

Did the family go to church?

Where, when, and how often?

What religious observance, if any, took place at home?

What ethnic groups influenced local society and farming practices, including land ownership? How?

How has geography and the natural environment influenced the layout of fields and buildings?

How has technology influenced the farm's environment?

What associations or clubs have been important to the farm's families, such as 4-H, FFA, card clubs, or other groups?

What recreational and leisure-time activities have been important to the people who have lived on the farm?

Have the farm's families participated in county and state fairs? In what respects?

How important have neighbors been to the farm in terms of mutual aid and friendships?

How have nearby communities affected farm life?

Economic Affairs

When did the farm become commercially rather then subsistence oriented?

Where did the owners market their crops, livestock, eggs, butter, and other products?

Why did the farm owners sell at these particular markets?

Have those markets changed? If so, why?

How has transportation changed over time in relation to marketing and social interaction?

Where did the owners spend their income?

What did they buy for farm and home?

How and why did those purchases change over time?

How profitable has the farm been from year to year?

When have economic hard times occurred and how have they affected the farm?

How has the farm survived those hard times?

When were the roads improved and by what method—plank, corduroy, sand, asphalt?

What financial institutions have affected this farm and how, such as local banks and the Federal Land Bank?

Have the farm's finances contributed to stability or instability of ownership or use?

Technological and Scientific Change

What was the earliest technology used on the farm for each specific crop?

How and why has that technology changed over time?

What was the significance of that technological change?

How has scientific change affected the farm?

When did the owners begin using organic and commercial fertilizers?

When did the operators begin using pesticides and herbicides?

When did the operators begin using hybrid seeds?

How have chemicals affected the farm economy and the land?

How did household technology change over time?

Farm Ownership and Labor

Who have been the owners?

Why has that ownership changed?

How were these changes made?

Has the farm been operated by tenants?

If so, who were they?

Were they share- or cash-rent tenants?

Why did tenants stay on or leave this farm?

What has been the relationship of this farm to hired labor?

Did this farm use slaves or indentured servants?

Were the slaves hired or owned?

What were the hiring or purchasing costs for slaves?

Has the farm used local hired labor? If so, why? What was the rate of pay?

Has this farm used migrant labor?

Were these migrants legal or illegal workers?

Has this farm aided or opposed the organization, that is, the unionization of labor?

How have wages changed over time?

Has the farm employed boys or girls on a seasonal basis?

If so, did they live on the farm?

Buildings and Gardens

What architectural styles can be found on the farm?

What do these styles tell about culture?

What do these styles tell about local resources?

What do these styles tell about perceptions of economy and efficiency, such as the use of bank or round barns?

When were these buildings constructed?

Where did the earliest building materials come from?

Were those materials wood, stone, or sod?

How has the architecture changed through the years?

Where were various barns, houses, and other buildings located at different periods?

What was the purpose of these buildings?

Where were the vegetable and herb gardens?

What seed varieties have been used over time and why?

Where have the flower gardens been located?

What landscape designs have been used?

Which flowers have been grown?

Education

What influence has the state agricultural extension service had on the farm?

What effect has the state agricultural college had on the farm?

Where did the children go to school?

Where was the country school?
When did it open?
When did it close for local consolidation?

Politics and Organizations

Were the people who lived on this farm politically active; if so, in what
    party?
Did these people join any reform organizations, such as the Grange,
    Farmers' Alliance, People's party, Nonpartisan League, Farmers'
    Holiday Association, Farm Bureau, or National Farmers' Union?
Did this organizational activity change their lives? If so, why?
How have the agricultural programs of the federal government af-
    fected the farm?

These questions are merely suggestions. Farm historians may not
choose to address all of them during the course of their research. Still,
these categories and questions will help the farm historian see the-
matic and topical relationships that can be pursued in research and
writing. Each category provides a place to start, but the researcher
should be sensitive to other questions that invariably will emerge
based on the sources being studied. Answering these questions will
help the historian to describe the history of the farm, show changes,
determine cause and effect and, most important, show the significance
of what took place there.

Writing agricultural history is exciting, challenging, and stimulat-
ing. It also involves hard work. Indeed, writing history accurately
never will be easy. In the beginning, however, the historian is not
ready to write. Indeed, much work needs to be completed before the
historian begins crafting a written account from the bits and pieces of
the past. If the research is done carefully and well, the final act of writing can be satisfying.

The keys to writing good history are to keep the research project
manageable and to be well prepared. One of the best ways to keep a
topic manageable is to limit its size. By choosing to write the history
of a farm the historian has limited the subject for research and writing
in a general way. The project has a beginning (so far as it can be determined) and an end (the present). It has chronological and physical
boundaries. As such the historian can give the topic intellectual control within the context of local, state, and national developments.

Many events and people influence a farm's history. The major
events and people associated with the farm may be separated by a considerable time. Take, for example, a farm located in the Western Re-

serve of Ohio and involved with dairying since 1818 when the first owner kept cows to supply milk for his family. In 1830 the farmer purchased more cows in order to expand production to convert the milk into cheese for shipment down the Ohio river to market in New Orleans. In 1860 the farmer bought an Ayshire bull to improve his herd. By the late nineteenth century the residents of Cleveland created a new demand for fluid milk, which the farm helped meet by converting its dairy cattle from a mixed breed to high producing, purebred Holsteins. In 1925 tuberculosis destroyed the herd, and although the farm owner rebuilt it and routinely tested his cows for the disease thereafter, full economic recovery did not occur until World War II. By the 1980s, a national surplus of dairy products and decreasing price supports encouraged the owner to take advantage of a federal program that enabled him to sell his dairy cattle and plant soybeans on land he had used for feed grains. These changes over nearly two centuries were influenced by developments in transportation, marketing, immigration, science, economics, and agricultural policy. Because the farm was engaged in many other activities during that time, the historian will face the challenge of keeping the story of the farm unified, sensible, and readable.

One sensible approach to handling this diffuse series of events would be to treat the general subject, that is, the farm, in a topical manner. In fact, a topical approach will enable even more manageability of the research project and give greater clarity and importance to the narrative. A topical approach also will help the historian eliminate information that, while interesting, does not substantially contribute to the story. Simply put, no one can recapture the past in its entirety. By taking a topical approach, the historian is making a conscious decision about what he or she believes to be the most important features of the farm's history. The topical pieces, such as founding the farm, technological change, social activities, farm architecture, changing boundaries, and crop and livestock production, become part of a larger mosaic that has broad meaning and significance. A topical technique also permits the historian to gain a thorough understanding of North American agricultural history. It enables the farm historian to make a contribution to knowledge by pursuing history from the ground up through systematic, rational study.

Indeed, by taking a fragment of the farm's past for close, careful study and by placing it in the context of state and national agricultural history, the research project moves beyond antiquarianism—the memory of things merely for their own sake—to history, that is, the memory of things to help preserve one's cultural heritage and to understand the meaning of the past.

When beginning to explore the history of a farm, then, the historian should compile a list of topics for study. These topics will not be all inclusive because the historian surely will add and delete from the list as the research progresses. With a farm selected for extensive historical study, a list of topics identified for intensive research, and a series of questions in mind, however, the farm historian is well prepared to begin gathering and evaluating historical evidence. In short, much exciting work has been completed. A more exhilarating experience awaits.

Chapter 2

WRITTEN RECORDS

The historian will use many sources of information about the past in researching and writing the history of an American farm. Some of these sources will be in written or printed form, such as family letters and experiment station bulletins. Some will be three-dimensional records, such as a log cabin, bank barn, or windmill. Others will be oral, resulting from interviews, and still others visual, such as photographs and maps. Each source can be important, and each will have its limitations. By using as many sources as possible the historian will gather a wide variety of information, some of which may be contradictory. The historian must attempt to use all of the sources effectively. In order to do so she or he is wise to start with the general and work toward the specific.

BOOKS

Farm historians may profit from first gaining a broad overview of the agricultural history of his or her state as well as national developments. By so doing, it will be possible to better judge the significance of the specific findings soon to come. In order to begin, the historian would do well to consult several books that will provide a basic summary of the field. For an overview of the most important social, economic, political, scientific, and technological developments in American agriculture from the occupation of the land by the Native Americans to the 1990s see R. Douglas Hurt, *American Agriculture: A Brief History* (Ames: Iowa State University Press, 1994) and David B. Danbom, *Born in the Country: A History of Rural America* (Baltimore: Johns Hopkins University Press, 1995). In addition, the farm historian should consult Willard W. Cochrane, *The Development of American Agriculture: A Historical Analysis*, 2nd ed. (Minneapolis: University of

Minnesota Press, 1993). This work surveys the main economic and technological features of American agriculture from the colonial period to the 1980s. In addition, anyone conducting research on the history of a farm should see John T. Schlebecker, *Whereby We Thrive: A History of American Farming, 1607–1972* (Ames: Iowa State University Press, 1975). This study emphasizes the history of science and technology in American agricultural history. Another source that can be useful is Walter Ebeling, *The Fruited Plain: The Story of American Agriculture* (Berkeley: University of California Press, 1979). The farm historian will also find these books helpful for gathering references to additional publications of possible interest.

Once having gained a basic understanding of the major developments in American agricultural history, farm historians should then turn their attention to the most important works relating to their state's agricultural and rural history. Although few state agricultural histories exist in book form, and most of those that have been written are rather dated or limited, it is worth determining whether such works exist. If a state agricultural history has been written it will serve as a guide to economic, social, and political developments that have closely affected agriculture on the local level, or, put differently, the agricultural developments that have been caused by the activities of individual farmers.

State agricultural histories often have been published by university presses or as bulletins of the state agricultural experiment stations. Occasionally, the farm historian will find a state agricultural history that has been privately printed. The farm historian should be most wary of the latter source, particularly if the study does not have documentation, such as foot- or endnotes, that enable independent verification of the facts. Books printed by academic or commercial presses probably will be more reliable because prior to publication each manuscript had the benefit of critical review by other experts in the field which helped the author to revise and strengthen the final work.

Sources on general American agricultural history can be obtained at or through the local public library. There, the historian should consult the card catalog or computer subject index for American or United States agriculture as well as for one's particular state. If the author or title of a book is already known, the entry can be found under these headings; otherwise subject indexes, though less reliable and comprehensive, may be helpful. If the historian lives near a college or university, the libraries at those institutions should be consulted for pertinent indexes and guides.

After reading several general agricultural histories and possibly a state agricultural history, the historian would be wise to visit the state historical society. These institutions exist to collect, preserve, and make available the history of the state. At the state historical society the historian should consult the card catalogs or computer files for books and articles about his or her state's agricultural history as well as for more specific studies that deal with various aspects of his or her county's agricultural history. To do so, the historian needs to check several subject heading files. Examples of the types of headings that might prove useful are agriculture; South Carolina agriculture; livestock; Iowa hog production; or New York, Otsego, County.

The card or computer catalog will provide the researcher with a more detailed list of sources about agricultural history at the state and county level. It will not necessarily supply a complete listing. In fact, most card and computer catalogs only list books. These catalogs often do not have cards with bibliographic citations for articles published in the state or county historical quarterlies, bulletins, or journals. Fewer still have cards for specialty journals such as *Agricultural History*, *Rural Sociology*, or the *Geographical Review*. The reasons for these omissions are that the continual updating of card and computer catalogs usually involves more staff time and expense than the state historical society can afford. This does not mean, however, that sources that have not been cataloged cannot be located. It merely means that farm historians must look further.

JOURNALS

Farm historians will benefit from consulting various published indexes that give further access to important secondary literature. These sources will deepen their understanding of state and local agricultural history. Such knowledge is essential if one is to fit a specific farm into the proper historical context and write its history.

The farm historian is wise to consult several indexes. The first should be *America: History and Life* (Santa Barbara: ABC-Clio, Inc., 1964–   ). This quarterly index provides bibliographical citations and annotations for the articles published in more than 2,100 scholarly journals. The historian should consult several categories in this index, such as agriculture, livestock, irrigation, and the name of one's particular state. This index is especially useful for learning about the agricultural and rural history articles concerning specific states and counties that have been published in the state historical society journals.

The farm historian can also profit from consulting the *Agricultural Index*, published from 1916 to 1964, which then became the *Biological and Agricultural Index*. This annual index contains titles to pertinent information published in both academic and government publications. Although the index probably can only be found at a college, university, or major public library, it can be helpful, and it merits consultation if it is available. It provides useful citations for publications by the United States Department of Agriculture.

The researcher should also consult George F. Thompson, *Index to Annual Reports of the United States Department of Agriculture for the Years 1838 to 1893, Inclusive*, USDA, *Bulletin no. 1*, 1896, which has a detailed subject index, as well as his *Index to Authors with Titles of Their Publications Appearing in the Documents of the United States Department of Agriculture, 1841–1897*, USDA, *Bulletin no. 4*, 1898. See also *List of Publications of the Agricultural Department, 1862–1902, with Analytical Index* (Washington, DC: Government Printing Office, 1904), which is an extensive index to the department's publications with citations and explanations of earlier indexes and includes a detailed section on the classification system of the superintendent of documents. This index was updated by Mabel G. Hunt, *List of Publications of the United States Department of Agriculture from January 1901 to December 1925* (Washington, DC: Government Printing Office, 1927). In addition the researcher should see the *Index to Publications of the Department of Agriculture* for the years 1901–1925, 1926–1930, 1931–1935, and 1936–1940.

The annual reports of the state departments of agriculture also include worthwhile information that will help put a farm's history in broad perspective. The publications of the state agricultural experiment stations also give important data about agriculture and rural life. Indeed, the experiment station publications provide information about important economic, social, scientific, and technological developments that have affected agriculture on the state and local levels and by so doing help the historian place the farm under study in the most meaningful historical context. The researcher should consult *List of Bulletins of the Agricultural Experiment Stations in the United States from the Establishment to the End of 1920* and the eleven supplements for 1924–1927 and 1930–1944. See also the cumulative indexes for the *Experiment Station Record* for the period 1889–1946. This publication succeeds the *Digest of the Annual Reports of the Agricultural Experiment Stations for 1888*. Since 1942, the *Bibliography of Agriculture* continues to provide access to experiment station research literature. It is published in hard copy by the National Agricultural Library or in electronic form, called CD-ROM, as AGRICOLA. This index lists agricultural articles published since 1970. Consequently the historian is wise to check the hard copy in order to be as thorough as possible.

Indeed, the publications of the state agricultural experiment stations can be particularly useful to any historian engaged in researching the history of a farm because this literature can help present broad historical context. The following two publications are illustrative: Bruce Melvin, "Rural Population, Tompkins and Schuyler Counties, New York, 1925," New York Agricultural Experiment Station, *Bulletin no. 487*, June 1929, and W. E. Grimes, R. S. Kifer, and J. A. Hodges, "The Effect of the Combined Harvester-Thresher on Farm Organization in Southwestern Kansas and Northwestern Oklahoma," Kansas Agricultural Experiment Station, *Circular 142*, 1928.

The *Social Sciences Index* and the *Humanities Index* also provide information about state and local agricultural and rural history. If an investigation deals with a farm or plantation that was once owned by a figure of national prominence, the researcher would do well to also consult the *Dictionary of American Biography* and the *Social Science Encyclopedia*.

Some scholarly journals have comprehensive indexes published every decade or so. The farm historian may consult, for example, the index for the *Journal of American History*, formerly the *Mississippi Valley Historical Review*, and the *Journal of Southern History*. *Agricultural History*, the journal of the Agricultural History Society, has been indexed from 1927 to 1989. These indexes, *Agricultural History: An Index, 1927–1976*, and *Agricultural History: An Updated Author, Title and Subject Index to the Journal, 1977–1989*, have been published by the Agricultural History Center at the University of California at Davis. The historian may also find pertinent articles about one's state or local agricultural and rural history in the annual cumulative indexes of other journals.

Important literature of the nineteenth century relating to agriculture can be located in *Poole's Index to Periodical Literature*. Twentieth century articles can be found in the *Readers Guide to Periodical Literature*. The latter source is particularly useful for locating articles in popular magazines. The *Magazine Index* also is helpful for this purpose. It contains more articles than the *Readers Guide*, and it is published on microfilm. These indexes will help the historian locate articles about general farming matters, such as analysis of agricultural legislation or discussions about the rural concerns of the past.

NEWSPAPERS

The farm historian is well advised next to consult various newspaper indexes in order to compile a more specific bibliography for later research. Some state historical societies have separate card catalogs that provide the precise source for specific information, such as Tobacco Production: Howard County, Missouri, see *Missouri Intelligencer* (Franklin), April 21, 1822. These indexes usually have been compiled by volunteers. Although these indexes are useful, the historian is properly cautioned to use them for introductory purposes only because they tend to be superficial rather than thorough compilations. One cannot assume that every reference to tobacco production in the *Missouri Intelligencer* has been noted for the card index. The historian would be imprudent to assume that these indexes are complete. Rather, they are a place to begin newspaper research. If one is to know precisely what the *Missouri Intelligencer* says about tobacco production in Howard County in 1822, she or he must look at each issue for that year. This procedure is not the easy way, but it is the only dependable way.

Professionals have compiled more contemporary but reliable newspaper indexes. During the Great Depression, for example, the Works Progress Administration (WPA) indexed many state newspapers. WPA newspaper indexes provide a quick reliable way to locate important agricultural information that pertains to the family farm. The WPA index for the *Cleveland Plain Dealer* contains an important guide to the efforts of the Rural Electrification Administration to furnish electricity to Ohio farms. The major national papers, such as the *New York Times* and *Washington Post*, as well as major regional newspapers, such as the *Chicago Tribune* and *Des Moines Register*, have also been indexed. Although these newspapers will not give specific information about a particular farm, their indexes will enable the historian to locate the information necessary to learn about national agricultural policy, such as the Payment-in-Kind Program, as well as regional events, like the 1967 milk strike by the National Farmers Organization (NFO), and other matters relating to contemporary agriculture. If a historian does not know which newspapers were published in the locale of the farm under study, those papers might be located in *American Newspapers, 1821–1936: A Union List of Files Available in the United States and Canada* (New York: H. W. Wilson, 1937) and *Newspapers in Microform: United States, 1948–72* (Washington, DC: Library of Congress, 1973). Some state historical societies have published newspaper indexes, such as Stephen Gutgesell, *Guide to Ohio Newspapers, 1793–1973* (Columbus: Ohio Historical Society, 1974). See also Karl J. R. Arndt and Mary Olson, *German-American Newspapers and Periodicals, 1732–1955* (New York: Johnson Reprint, 1965) and *The German Language Press of the Americas* [1732–1968] (Munich: Verlag Dokumentation, 1976). Local libraries may have pertinent newspapers on microfilm, or the interlibrary loan librarian can acquire them for the researcher.

Despite these indexes the thorough historian will want to consult all of the newspapers available—town and county, daily and weekly—for the entire period under study. If, for example, the history of the farm begins in 1800, and ceases in 1950 because of urban sprawl, the historian needs to read every available local paper for that time period in order to adequately understand the agricultural issues important to the county, town, and neighborhood during the course of that 130-year period. Newspaper indexes are essential, but the historian can not rely on them completely. Newspaper research is slow but often interesting work and the rewards for the farm historian are immeasurable.

COUNTY HISTORIES

The historian who studies a specific American farm will also want to consult county histories. These sources can be valuable, if judiciously used. During the late nineteenth and early twentieth centuries, several commercial publishers compiled county histories to which the residents were invited to contribute a family history—for a price. By taking subscriptions as well, the publisher hoped to make a profit. Generally, the publisher accepted the contributions of its subscribers at face value. These histories primarily are devoted to local boosterism and achievement. They are not analytical; frequently they are inaccurate. Even so, the careful historian will find them valuable because they often contain information about local agricultural history that cannot be found elsewhere. This fact, of course, leads to the matter of verification. All historians are compelled to make judgments on their knowledge of the past. If, given the secondary reading that the historian has conducted on state and national agricultural history, and given what he or she knows about agriculture in the county, a particular unverifiable statement of fact seems reliable then the historian should cautiously accept it, but acknowledge the tentative nature of the conclusion.

County histories also can provide useful biographical and family information. The farm historian ought to realize, however, that most local farmers did not pay to be included in a county history. It is a mark of good fortune, and the subject's economic circumstances, to find the person or family one is seeking. At the very least these histories will enable farm historians to gain a better understanding of a county's agricultural practices, markets, and related affairs. Still, it is well to remember that these histories primarily emphasized local elites. Most farmers and their farms were not included because they could not or would not pay the monetary price to do so.

During the late twentieth century, local history gained legitimacy as a field of study for professional historians. As a result, town and county histories often became more thorough and reliable. These histories usually contain valuable information about local agricultural and marketing practices. If the historian cannot locate a county history on the library shelf or card or computer catalog, he or she should consult C. S. Peterson, *Consolidated Bibliography of County Histories in Fifty States in 1961, Consolidated 1935–1961*, 2d ed. (Baltimore: Genealogical Pub. Co., 1963) and Marion J. Kaminkow, ed., *United States Local Histories in the Library of Congress*, 5 vols. (Baltimore: Magna Carta, 1975).

∽

County histories can provide excellent background about local agricultural practices. The following passage from *Past and Present of Hardin County Iowa* (Indianapolis: B. F. Bowder & Co., 1911) gives the researcher essential information about gender, technology, marketing, labor, soil conservation, and romanticism in relation to farming in the county from the mid-nineteenth to the early twentieth century.

The earliest breaking of Hardin county virgin soil by white men was in the autumn of 1849, in what is now Union township, by Greenberry Haggin. . . . Then all, on every hand, was one "green glad solitude." Today not an acre of land can be found not devoted to some branch of agricultural Industry. . . .

At an early date there were numerous marshes within some sections of Hardin county, but today these spots are among the finest corn and grain and grass-producing portions of the goodly domain.

Ditching, tilling and general cultivation of the surface has wrought great changes for the better. The pioneer farm implements were necessarily rude and farming was conducted in a slipshod manner. The old-time "bar-share" plow was employed. In many cases the wooden mould-board was still used. Frequently the pioneer chanced to have a daughter old enough to better handle the lines than a younger son, hence she would "drive the plow" for her father. She wore a dress of homespun, "buttoned up behind," "leather boots," etc. In corn planting time she used to drop the corn and cover it with a hoe, and it grew just as large as though planted by a horse, a check-row planter, operated by the male sex!

For wheat, the land was prepared same as for corn, and harrowed with a wooden toothed "drag," or smoothed with a brush drag. It was then sowed broadcast by hand, at the rate of a bushel and a quarter to an acre, and again harrowed in with a brush drag. At harvest time the expert cradler was paid big wages and much sought after, up and down the country, as was also a good stacker. The average farmer knew how to swing a grass scythe and with it the first hay in Hardin county was made. Three cradlers would cut about ten acres a day, so it will be seen that actually the cost of harvesting was not much in excess of that of today, but it took longer to secure a harvest and men could not always be had to do the work. One binder was expected to keep up with the cradler. The first threshing was done either by means of a "flail" or by horses or oxen treading out the grain from the straw, and they slowly traversed a circle. Then the fanning-mill agent got in his work and a few of his "wonderful wind machines" were sold in each township. With these the wheat was cleaned for milling and seed purposes.

These methods have long since passed from the face of the earth. The mowing machine, and reaper, and planter, and corn cutter and steam thresher and gang, riding plow, all made of steel and iron, have taken the place of these rude contrivances. Men can now do more work on a given tract of land in a day and can produce more and finer crops. The markets have changed and prices for the last decade have been never so high and, as a general rule, the Hardin county farmer is king of the situation and while his town brother is glad for his trade, he heaves a long sigh and wishes now that he had remained a farmer. Now over the once broad prairies of this section of Iowa can be found farmhouses with palace appearance; with hot and cold water, with electric lights and a daily paper each morning to read. . . . The richness of the soil makes it useless to pay fancy prices for artificial fertilizers. Proper tilling and the growth of clover, turned back to corn every five years, keeps the soil in splendid shape for the production of big crops.

ॐ

DISSERTATIONS AND THESES

Many master's degree theses and Ph.D. dissertations provide valuable information about state and county history that will be helpful to anyone researching and writing the story of a farm. The college or university where the work was completed can be depended upon to have copies. These can sometimes can be obtained through the interlibrary loan service of the public library. Sometimes the author of these research projects deposit copies in the appropriate local library. Often the state historical society will have copies of these works as well. Although M.A. theses usually are available only from the originating institution, guides have been published such as Homer E. Socolofsky, *Kansas History in Graduate Study: A Bibliography of Theses and Dissertations* (Topeka: Kansas State Historical Society, 1970). The historian is wise to ask the local public, college, or historical society libraries about the possible existence of relevant bibliographies.

Dissertations for the Ph.D. usually involve more extensive research than M.A. theses. Happily, they are also more easily available. Dissertations written from 1873 to 1980 at American and Canadian universities can be located in publications edited by Warren F. Kuehl: *Dissertations in History, 1970–June 1980* (Santa Barbara: ABC-Clio, 1985) and *Dissertations in History, 1873–1970*, 2 vols. (Lexington: University of Kentucky Press, 1965–72). The subject index enables relatively quick determination of whether research has been done on one's project. In addition, each year University Microfilms International publishes *Dissertation Abstracts*, an annotated abstract with order numbers for all dissertations completed that year at participating institutions. These dissertations can be purchased in paperback or microfilm form. Usually universities that participate in this service do not lend their dissertations through interlibrary loan. University Microfilms also publishes the comprehensive *Dissertation Index* as well as special dissertation bibliographies for each state. The bibliographies are free and can be ordered from University Microfilms International, 300 North Zeeb Road, Ann Arbor, Michigan 48106. If the historian finds a reference to a dissertation that seems likely to be useful and cannot get it through interlibrary loan, he or she should see if it is available through University Microfilms. This service is particularly beneficial for researchers who cannot travel to the appropriate university library across the state or nation. *Dissertation Abstracts* can also be consulted at some research libraries via computer on-line or CD-ROM services.

CITY DIRECTORIES

The farm historian should not forget to consult directories for nearby cities, particularly for the nineteenth century. These directories provide listings for various merchants and tradesmen and advertisements for many agricultural commission men and manufacturers. City directories can help the historian understand the available markets that affected production on the farm. These directories often were revised annually, but, while they provide an overview of the agricultural orientation of the city, they are by no means complete. To identify early city directories, see Dorothea N. Spear, *Bibliography of American Directories through 1860* (Worcester, MA: American Antiquarian Society, 1961). These sources can be used for both general and specific agricultural information, but not for definitive statements of fact.

PUBLIC DOCUMENTS

Guides to federal and state documents that may prove helpful to farm historians are the following:

Checklist of United States Public Documents, 1789–1909; Catalog of Public Documents of the United States, 1893–1940; William W. Buchanan and Edna A. Kanely, eds., *Cumulative Subject Index to the Monthly Catalog of United States Government Publications, 1900–1971;* and, after that latter date, the *Monthly Catalog of United States Government Publications.* Another important index is the *U.S. Serial Set Index* for publications of the federal government from 1787 to 1969. *The Annual Index to Congressional Publications and Public Laws* provides similar information for publications since 1970.

An introduction to state documents can be found in R. R. Bowker, ed., *State Publications: A Provisional List of the Official Publications of the Several States of the United States from their Organization* for documents before 1900. See also William A. Jenkins, ed., *Collected Public Documents of the States: A Checklist for Sources to 1947.* Contemporary state documents can be identified in the Library of Congress's *Monthly Checklist of State Publications.* For the possibility of local government documents that pertain to agriculture and rural life see J. G. Hodgson, ed., *Official Publications of American Counties: A Union List*, and A. D. Manvel, ed., *Checklist of Basic Manuscript Documents.*

UNPUBLISHED SOURCES

Having gained a broad overview of American, state, and local agricultural history, a researcher is well prepared for intensive research in unpublished primary resources, such as letters, diaries, probate records, deeds, tax rolls, abstracts, and census schedules. The historian may already have a collection of papers that directly relate to the farm under study. If not, the researcher may be able to locate such papers, such as account books and letters, that the owners of the farm have written through the years. Or, the investigator may be able to find similar papers from a nearby farm or papers of important people who were engaged in agriculture and who lived nearby. These sources will help the farm historian better understand the nature of agriculture at various times during the life of the farm.

If one does not personally have a collection of papers that relate to the farm, this does not mean that those sources do not exist. Such papers may be in the possession of friends, relatives, or various past owners or tenants of the farm. They should be contacted about the project, and asked for permission to use their papers. If neither friends nor family or others have papers relating to the history of the farm, the public library may have such a manuscript collection. The historian would be wise to contact the local or county historical society as well as the state historical society about such papers. In all probability the state historical society will have several collections of agricultural manuscripts that will provide direct information about the farm or about agriculture in the particular neighborhood or county of the farm at one or more points in time.

When writing to the state historical society it is best to address your letter to the "Archivist" or "Curator of Manuscripts." Either an archivist or manuscript specialist will answer it, usually quite promptly. In your letter, it is helpful to be as specific as possible about the names of the people who might have left papers, the county and location of the farm, and the time period of concern. The person who answers the inquiry probably will mention several manuscript collections that merit research. At this point you may either need to go to the society to conduct research, or hire someone to do it. Some institutions will

Land records are important for anyone writing the history of a farm. This Homestead Certificate was issued by the General Land office to Gilbert Kreider on February 21, 1893. It gives the exact location of the farm by quarter section, township, and range. *Kansas State Historical Society.*

photocopy and send a limited amount of material, usually for a fee. Although it is always best to conduct your own research, state historical societies invariably have a list of people who are willing to conduct research for a fee. If you cannot make a necessary trip yourself, ask for recommendations of researchers to use for your project.

If you travel to the state historical society or other institution to examine a manuscript collection, upon arrival ask to see the archivist or manuscripts specialist with whom you have been corresponding. Indeed, it is best to arrange an appointment well in advance. At this meeting you can discuss your project more fully and gain additional information. In all likelihood the archivist or manuscripts specialist will show you the card or computer catalog which you can use to locate papers. Some collections will have printed guides that generally tell you the contents of specific folders in the manuscript collection. Once you decide which papers to scrutinize you will request the papers on a call slip and an archivist will bring them to you. These papers may be in several forms, such as letters, lists of lands or slaves owned, property inventories, or diaries. Personal papers, account books, and letters can be particularly useful for collecting information about specific agricultural facts and the nature of life on the farm.

COUNTY RECORDS

Sometimes local government records will be found in manuscript collections. Usually, however, these records will be housed in the state archives or remain with the originating agency, often in the county courthouse. These records include probate pockets (a collection of all legal materials that involved settlement of the estate, including property valuations and inventories). Property valuations and inventories can indicate the standard of living on the farm at the death of a particular owner. In the county treasurer's office, tax records will list the property and the valuations for the various owners of the farm.

Wills and deeds also are important resource materials. Wills, for example, provide a good general description of the amount of farm property conveyed and stipulate how it is to be used and whether that use will eventually change as upon the death of a wife who had inherited one-third of the farm to support herself, but upon whose death it became the property of the eldest son. Wills also show the division of the property, livestock, and slaves. If wills that pertain to the farm are not included in family papers, the researcher may find them at the county courthouse. The clerk of the probate court can help locate the records for the person in question. Sometimes these records will have been turned over to the state archives, which may be an independent agency or part of the state historical society.

ॐ

The following will provides a particularly good example of the information that can be gained about a farm from such documents. It makes evident many of the different kinds of information that a historian can obtain from such sources. This Missouri farm will is dated October 6, 1825.

The last will and testament of Cumberland Snell, Columbia township Boone County.

I Cumberland Snell, considering the uncertainty of the mortal life, and being of sound mind and memory (helped by Almighty God for the same) do make, public and declare this my last will and testament, in manner and form following (that is to say)

I give and bequeath unto my beloved wife Elizabeth Snell, the home tract of land which is the Northwest quarter section Number two Range twelve & township forty eight with all and singular appertuances thereunto belonging or in anywise appertaining, as also all the stock of every description, and all the farming utensils the wagon included, household and kitchen furniture together with all my slaves (whose names are as follows) Sam, Lucy, Sharlotte, and Henderson, Phebe, Emily, Hannah, Washington, Baker, Ben and Sarah with their fifteen increase to remain with her in peaceable possession, during her life or widowhood, in the event of her marrying again, it is my wish, and in fact my will that the property thus left her should be by my Executors advertised and sold at public vendue according to law, the money accruing therefrom to be equally divided among my children (all of my children that may be under age at the time of her second marriage if that event should take place). I wish and will that the county court should appoint for each of them a suitable person or persons to be their guardians, until such child or children should marry, or come of age. My object for willing the above property as I have above, was that all my children should remain with their mother and be supported, raised and educated off of the produce of the place, the increase of the stock and the labor of the slaves. I appoint her my said beloved wife guardian to all my children until the youngest comes of age . . . or if she should die or marry as second time, in such event my Executor will do as above directed.

Then I give and bequeath to my eldest daughter Mary Snell one half quarter section of land (to wit) the west half of the Southeast quarter of section twenty-six in township forty nine of range twelve as described in certificate 782. . . .

Then I give and bequeath to my Eldest son John Ashby Snell one quarter section of land (to wit) the South West quarter of section Number thirty five in township forty nine of Range twelve as described in certificate 158. . . .

Then I give and bequeath to my daughter Albina Snell one quarter section of land (to wit) the South east quarter of Section Eighteen in township forty eight of Range twelve as described in certificate No. 1082, moreover I hereby authorize my executor to sell and legally convey the last described quarter section of land, and appropriate the money arising from the sale of the same to purchase another tract of land for my said daughter Albina Snell if they think advisable so to do at any time before she comes of age or marrys. . . .

Then I give and bequeath to my daughter Francis Snell the home place at her mothers death. . . .

I further will and authorize my Executors to sell and legally convey, two lots of land one containing forty acres and the other Eleven lying and being among the out-lots of the town of Columbia if they think it advisable. . . .

❧

Deeds also provide important information about property bought and sold. These records contain precise descriptions of the land conveyed note the price paid for it, the parties to the sale, and the date. As in the case of probate records, deeds can be located in the county courthouse, although the precise offices may vary, such as the office of the county clerk, treasurer, or clerk of the probate court. Or, deeds may be located at the state archives, if these documents are not part of the family papers or manuscript collections. Usually, the appropriate deed can be located by using the County Registry of Deeds located with the county clerk. These registries include two essential indexes: a "Grantee Index," which lists alphabetically the names of those who purchased property and a "Grantor Index," which lists the sellers. These indexes usually are bound in volumes that cover registrations over a period of several years.

The farm historian needs to know the name of the person who owned a tract of land and the approximate year that he or she purchased it. The Grantee Index will show from whom the land was purchased, date of purchase, general location of the land, and the volume

and page number of the actual deed. Next, the researcher should locate the seller or grantor in the Grantor Index to cross check from
whom he or she purchased the land. If the Registry of Deeds is complete, the historian should be able to work backward to locate the
original deed from the Public Land Office or a speculator. One way to
begin is to locate the last known deed and work backward from that
point. If a Registry of Deeds cannot be located the probate records will
show how and when the land was willed.

A visit to the county treasurer's or assessor's office to study the abstract of the farm can also prove worthwhile. An abstract is a history
of all land acquisitions and sales that pertain to the farm. Every piece
of land has a legal history that can be traced. Land abstracts will show
whether liens have been imposed on the property as well as the names
of all mortgagees and mortgagors. Name changes by the land's owners will also be documented in the abstract, and it will show foreclosures and bankruptcies. The abstract will also indicate the location of
rights-of-way for roads and railroads, some of which may no longer
exist.

The reports of the rural school district located in the county courthouse or state historical society also may prove useful for understanding the educational and social life of the children who lived on
the farm over time. If a church is or was located near the farm, its records, anniversary brochures, and programs may be helpful as well.
The official records of the church may be located in the church itself,
at the particular denomination's archives, the public library, or county
or state historical society. Two excellent books that will provide an introduction to the research and writing of school and church history
are: Ronald E. Butchart, *Local Schools: Exploring Their History* (Nashville: American Association for State and Local History, 1986) and
James P. Wind, *Places of Worship: Exploring Their History* (Nashville:
American Association for State and Local History, 1990).

CENSUS RECORDS

In 1790 the first federal census was taken. Each decade thereafter
until 1850, the census recorded only the names and addresses of heads
of households; the other members of the family were not identified,
only enumerated by sex in age groups. Beginning in 1850, however,
the census takers listed the names of all free persons along with age,
sex, color, occupation, value of property, and birthplace (state or coun-

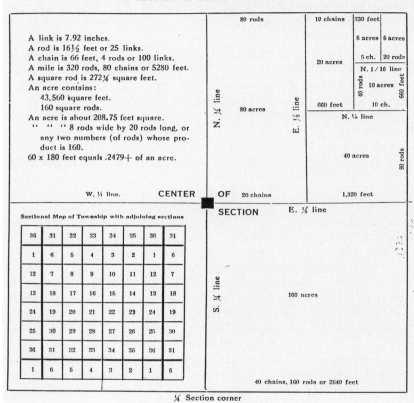

TITLE EXAMINER'S AID

Boone County, Iowa, is situated in the Central part of Iowa and consists of Townships 82–83–84–85, North of Base Line established on a parallel with the mouth of St. Francis River, Arkansas, and Ranges 25–26–27–28, West of Fifth Principal Meridian which is established from the mouth of the Arkansas River.

A SECTION OF LAND—640 ACRES

A link is 7.92 inches.
A rod is 16½ feet or 25 links.
A chain is 66 feet, 4 rods or 100 links.
A mile is 320 rods, 80 chains or 5280 feet.
A square rod is 272¼ square feet.
An acre contains:
    43,560 square feet.
    160 square rods.
An acre is about 208.75 feet square.
  " " " 8 rods wide by 20 rods long, or
    any two numbers (of rods) whose pro-
    duct is 160.
60 x 180 feet equals .2479+ of an acre.

In 1785, the Land Act provided for the survey and sale of the public domain. Various land laws thereafter modified the amount of land that an individual could purchase from the federal government, but the original surveying principles remained. Surveyors divided public lands into sections containing 640 acres, half sections of 320 acres, and quarter sections of 160 acres. Thirty-six numbered sections compose a township. *Author's Collection.*

Land Abstracts can help the local historian trace the history of a farm. This abstract was prepared for Wallace Farley near Ogden, Iowa, on October 15, 1889, and it was updated on March 15, 1889, because of an acquisition or sale of land. *Author's Collection.*

try). In 1880 the enumerator also recorded the birthplace (state or country) of the mother and father of each person.

While these records are important, the historian needs to remember that the census takers commonly misspelled some names, omitted others, and made errors. In addition, the names are not listed alphabetically but rather in the order in which the census taker visited the households in his area. Sometimes, indexes to various censuses will have been compiled by volunteers and located at the state historical societies. Individual names can be located relatively easily by using Soundex indexes, if available, which are phonetic spellings of surnames followed by the given name of heads of households. The National Archives has prepared a Soundex index for all households in the 1880 census in which there was a child ten years old or younger. The Soundexes for the 1900 and 1910 censuses include all families.

In 1840, federal government took the first agricultural census as part of the sixth population census of the United States. Although it did not include a wide variety of categories and the accuracy of the tabulations can be questioned, it at least gives an approximation of the statistical status of farming in America at that time. Thereafter, until 1950, the census of agriculture was included in the decennial census. In 1925, 1935, and 1945, however, a separate mid-decade census of agriculture was taken, and continued every five years from 1954 to 1974.

In 1976, Congress authorized the agricultural census to coincide with the economic census for manufacturing, mining, construction, transportation, retail and wholesale trade, and the service industry. That change meant the agricultural census would be conducted cyclically for the years ending in 2 and 7. The agricultural census provides excellent information about farming, such as tabulations for crops, livestock, and cash value of acreage and implements as well as summaries of population, technology, and other farm-related matters. This multivolume series includes coverage of each state and a summary volume. The information recorded in the population census has changed over time. In 1860, for example, the value of personal property was added and in 1880 the enumerator ask farmers whether they were owners or cash or share tenants.

Although no census is precise, each provides a reliable overview of American society at the time it was taken. The census particularly is valuable for agricultural information, such as the amount of improved and unimproved land owned, farm value, and crops and livestock produced. In the published census, county by county aggregations of data can provide a good understanding of agriculture in the neighborhood of the farm under study. The schedules or information sheets used by the enumerators to record information are particularly important for agricultural research, because the data found there is only summarized in the printed censuses. These schedules have been microfilmed and are available for study at public, state historical society, and college and university libraries and at the National Archives in Washington, D.C. These schedules are currently open through 1920. All census schedules are kept from public scrutiny for seventy-two years to protect the privacy of individuals. The census schedules for 1890, however, were destroyed by a fire at the Bureau of the Census.

The manuscript schedules are in four parts, and all farm historians can profittably use three of them beginning in 1840. If research deals with a farm in the South all four ought to be consulted. One schedule is for population, that is, names of heads of households, their members, and occupations. A second schedule lists agricultural information, such as improved and unimproved acres and crops and livestock raised, machinery owned, and household production, such as butter and cheese. A third schedule records the name of slave owners, the number of slaves held, their sex and age, and sometimes their names as well as the number of cabins provided for them. The fourth schedule records manufacturers and notes names, number of employees and production, such as pounds of pork packed, number of tobacco casks shipped, tons of hemp made into rope, or the amount of flour milled in the major towns. When indexes are not available the historian can save much time by knowing the townships where the farm is located. Then, the researcher locates those schedules for the appropriate county and township and works through the pages until names of concern are located. Published census information beginning in 1850 with the *Federal Census of Population, Agriculture and Manufacturing* provides a statistical overview of farming and rural life on a county basis.

Occasionally, states conducted censuses between decennial years. County sheriffs or designated officials often were the enumerators. These printed results can be difficult to locate, but the results often were published in local newspapers.

FEDERAL RECORDS

Federal records relating to agriculture, other than the census, can provide a broader framework for the history of a farm, particularly in relation to agricultural policy. Since the federal government did not become involved with agricultural policy, other than tariff regulations until the late 1920s, the farm historian will likely be most concerned with USDA branches or independent agencies that emerged later, such as the Soil Conservation Service, Agricultural Stabilization and Conservation Service, Resettlement Administration, Agricultural Adjustment Administration, or Farmers Home Administration. The records of these agencies will be located at the National Archives or at one of its regional branches. The staff at the National Archives publish guides to the collections, such as *Guide to Records in the National Archives—Central Plains Region* (Washington, DC: National Archives and Records Administration, 1989). The best way to locate information of this sort, however, is to write to the National Archives or the regional branch and explain the nature of the research project. The historian should be as specific as possible about the information that he or she would like to find or the subject that is under study. Perhaps, for example, part of the farm under study became government property under the Resettlement Administration and eventually became part of a National Grassland. The National Archives will have the records under the category of Land Utilization Projects. Or, perhaps the farm received government aid during the Great Depression as part of the Agricultural Adjustment Administration's crop reduction program for cotton, wheat, or hogs. The records for these programs will be located at the National Archives. Of course, much secondary literature exists about federal agricultural programs such as these but determined farm historians may wish to pursue intensive study of these primary sources to add another dimension to the research project. Anyone who cannot travel to the National Archives to conduct research can hire a researcher from a list provided by that research institution.

The historian who has undertaken the task of writing a history of a farm will not necessarily use all of these sources. These sources, however, do offer a sensible place to begin. They provide specific information about the farm and the historical context necessary to give purpose and meaning to its story.

SUGGESTED READINGS

The best guide for the practice of local history in general is David E. Kyvig and Myron A. Marty, *Nearby History: Exploring the Past Around You* (Nashville: American Association for State and Local History, 1982). For a guide to selected manuscript collections and repositories see the *Directory of Archives and Manuscript Repositories in the United States* (Washington, DC: National Historical Publications and Records Commission, 1978). The *National Union Catalog of Manuscript Collec-*

tions, published periodically by the Library of Congress also provides information about manuscripts in its collection. See also the *Guide to the National Archives of the United States* (Washington, DC: National Archives and Record Service, 1974). The National Archives also publishes guides to specific collections.

Other useful studies include: Philip C. Brooks, *Research in Archives: The Use of Unpublished Primary Sources* (Chicago: University of Chicago Press, 1969); Robert G. Barrows, "The Manuscript Federal Census: Source for 'New' Local History," *Indiana Magazine of History* 69 (September 1973): 181–92; Lutz Berkner, "The Use and Misuse of Census Data for the Historical Analysis of Family Structure," *Journal of Interdisciplinary History* 4 (Spring 1975): 721–38; *State and Local Censuses: An Annotated Bibliography* (1944; Reprinted, Westport, CT: Greenwood Press, 1976); and Nancy Sahli, "Local History Manuscripts: Sources, Uses, and Preservation," *Technical Leaflet 115*, American Association for State and Local History, 1979.

Chapter 3

ORAL HISTORY

Written materials, such as letters, diaries, newspapers, and census records, are important sources for the farm historian, but oral history can provide an exciting further dimension to his or her work. Simply put, oral history can give the historian access to unrecorded information. Used critically and carefully, it can be an exceptionally useful method for historical research. Often people do not leave written records because they are unaccustomed to keeping diaries or writing letters. Yet many preserve activities in their mind. A skillful interviewer can help a person recall events and put experiences into words. The memory, of course, plays tricks, particularly if a considerable amount of time has passed from an occurrence to its recollection. Consequently, the interviewer must be more than just a listener, tape recorder operator, or notetaker. She or he must be an inquiring historian with the ability to stimulate recollections by appropriate questions. The oral historian also needs the capacity for critical evaluation as well as the skill and knowledge to corroborate what was said, and if not, know when to use or reject it.

GENERAL CONSIDERATIONS

Oral history provides access to the recent as well as the distant past. Oral history deals with events that written documents usually do not address, such as who planted what crops, when, where, and why? Or, who grazed what livestock, when, where, and why? Often, oral history can complement and expand the written record. Oral history also might prove the written record incorrect. Certainly, oral history can help the farm historian interpret his or her research, that is, give it meaning and significance during the writing process.

If family members, such as husbands, wives, brothers, sisters, sons, daughters, nephews and nieces, tenants, or new or long-time owners lived on the farm, they become appropriate subjects for interviews about their recollections and experiences related to the operation of the farm. Grandparents, uncles, aunts, and cousins, or anyone who ever owned or worked on the farm can be important resources for historical research. Oral history is better done sooner than later, particularly if people important to the project are advancing in age or are ill. Still, oral interviews ought to be left until the historian has a solid background in the area's agricultural history and some knowledge of the history of the farm gained from written sources.

In general, the practice of oral history involves recording an individual's recollections of past events. The researcher conducts an interview designed to gain general relevant historical information as well as to reconstruct specific events with which the respondent had personal experience. In either case, the prudent historian does not approach this research methodology in a haphazard fashion. Oral history can provide important knowledge and insight about the past, and it can be fun, but it requires considerable preparation and careful effort.

The effective researcher first plans the oral history project carefully. The skilled practice of oral history as a research tool means more than simply asking questions. It is not difficult, but it requires forethought, planning, and sensitivity as well as perseverance, accuracy, and thoroughness when transcribing the tapes and analyzing the results. In addition, the social, educational, economic, and political backgrounds of the person to be interviewed, as well as of the historian, need to be considered because each will influence the questions asked and the answers given. Moreover, oral history as a research methodology provides more than facts. Facial expressions, vocal emphasis, and body language of the respondent can provide an important context for the oral statements.

The researcher should consider oral history both broadly and narrowly, that is, generally and specifically regarding the information to be gained. General information to be gathered might include a perspective on the agricultural economy, the value of the local Grange, or the importance of neighborhood social activities at the country church. Specific information might involve the reconstruction of events that the respondent experienced firsthand, such as participating in a milk strike, forming a rural electric cooperative, or establishing a roadside market.

Oral history projects ought to be realistically designed in terms of time and money. It is axiomatic that research projects always take longer to complete than originally anticipated. In this regard, the farm historian will do well to decide the number of people to be interviewed as well as determine the time period to be covered with each respondent. Where do the respondents live? Does age or ill health threaten to make the interview less than reliable? Simply put, this research must be systematic. The researcher is wise to determine in advance the important questions to be asked yet remain flexible enough to go where the interviewee takes the historian. The researcher, of course, sets the scope of the interview, but resiliency is a virtue as well as a necessity in this type of historical research.

The planning of the project will be aided by the researcher's knowledge of the history of state and local agriculture gained from books, articles, bulletins, manuscripts, newspapers, and census schedules. Effective researchers endeavor to use oral history to provide new information rather than to duplicate what is already known. If the researcher does not live in the neighborhood of the farm but travels to see it, he or she may establish contact with potential interviewees in the area. The local librarian, newspaper editor, or postmaster or postmistress may be able to provide the names of local residents who know something about the farm. If someone besides a family member owns the farm, notice of arrival is likely to improve results, at least more so than if one is dealing with a relative who probably will be supportive of this research project. The researcher also can use the visit to establish contacts with others not originally included on the research agenda, if this is merited. In addition, a preliminary visit will help respondents get to know the researcher and to feel at ease, and it will encourage them to think about the information sought by the researcher.

Many questions can be planned and written down, but the wise researcher allows for spontaneity on the part of the respondent. Moreover, experienced interviewers do not expect precise answers to questions about a specific event that occurred many years in the past. When conducting interviews it is best to make questions clear and open-ended. Skilled oral historians try to be as specific as possible without emphasizing factual matter such as dates. For example, they do not ask, "On what date did the Rural Electrification Administration bring electricity to the farm?" Rather, they ask, "How did electricity change the farm?" Or, "During the New Deal which agricultural programs of the Roosevelt administration most affected the farm?" Or, "Why did you decide to participate in the program of the Agricultural Adjustment Administration?" The key is to be sufficiently, but not too, specific. The questions should permit flexibility for both the respondent and the interviewer. It is best to avoid questions that require lengthy, complicated answers. At the same time, questions that can be answered with "yes" or "no" may lead to disappointing, undetailed responses. Remember that questions missed may be addressed at the end of the interview and that follow-up interviews may be necessary.

Practice interviews with family members and friends can help one prepare. This enables the researcher to learn how to manage an interview, direct the questions toward a particular goal, or adjust to the flow of the interview. With practice, the historian can learn to ask questions that are clear, and sufficiently open-ended to enable the collection of useful information. Such sessions also allow the researcher to learn to operate the tape recorder efficiently and unobtrusively as well as to take notes while someone answers questions.

Having prepared to conduct interviews, the researcher does well to begin with willing family members, if the farm remains in the family. This technique has several merits. It enables the historian to begin this form of research with those with whom he or she feels most at ease and who feel comfortable with the interviewer. By so doing, less enthusiastic family members, relatives, or friends might be coaxed into granting an interview. Such interviews also enable the historian to gain experience with interview techniques and, thereby, become more skilled before interviewing strangers.

After the historian has obtained permission to conduct an interview, he or she also should receive written permission from the respondent to quote from it. Securing permission is both an ethical practice and a legal protection, if you plan to publish your history. A letter of release should also give the historian the authority to deposit the tapes and transcript in a manuscript collection or library. If a respondent is hesitant to sign such a release document, get his or her oral permission on tape before proceeding. Otherwise, an important interview might be unusable and lost forever for purposes of historical research. If the farm historian does not receive permission to quote from an interview, however, the researcher can still paraphrase the essential information. The historian also must be prepared for the respondent to request that the taped interview be withheld from use for a period of time or until after his or her death. This may happen if sensitive family experiences or disagreements relating to the farm have occurred, such as arguments over inheritance, money, marketing, or politics.

The farm historian will do well to remember that a basic difference between oral and written sources is that oral interviews enable understanding of the *meaning* of events while written documents stress the *details*, such as what happened, when, where, and why. A land patent, for example, will give the date that the original owner received title to federal land, but an interview will indicate the significance of the foreclosure sale to the people who lived on that land a century later. Suppose a researcher is conducting research about a farm in California or New Mexico where the land originally was granted by the Spanish governor in 1800 and confirmed by Mexican authorities in 1825 and by American officials in 1860. These transactions can be traced with legal documents, if they are extant. From these papers the historian can learn the names of the landowners and the size, description, and boundary of the land grant. By following the history of the possession of the land through wills and deeds, the historian can trace how the land grant expanded or contracted as well as the price paid for new purchases or received from the sales of tracts from the original grant. Suppose, however, that in the mid-twentieth century a considerable portion of the land grant was sold or divided in some way, such as through probate. The paper documents often fail to reveal why this happened. Did economic misfortune force the owner to sell the farm? Did the family fight about which son or daughter should inherit the land, which, in turn, caused a court battle that ultimately changed the inheritance? Questions such as these can be addressed by using oral history. By interviewing family members, distant relatives, close friends, or neighbors about the event, matters of motive, nuance, and behavior can give meaning to the precise facts in the legal documentation.

If a controversial matter has affected the history of a farm, be sure to get both sides of the story, if possible. Disagreements among family members or landowners and tenants are common, and the oral historian is obligated to collect as much information as possible in order to interpret and write the history of a farm. Similarly, the farm may have shifted from emphasizing dairying to soybeans based on matters of economics, time, gender, and labor, among other considerations, but it may not have occurred with family harmony or unanimity. Yet, the decision was an important event in the history of the farm. If major disputes have occurred, the oral historian needs to learn about them, evaluate their context, and determine their significance.

Oral history can provide essential information about daily life on the farm, organization of the household, and social and cultural values. In some cases, oral histories may provide the only documentation for a particular period of a farm's history. In most cases, however, oral histories and written records are best combined. This enables the historian to draw on a variety of sources when writing the history of a farm.

The researcher may improve his or her interviewing technique by reviewing one interview before conducting another. This review will enable the historian to determine whether a follow-up interview might be necessary and, if so, what topics should be discussed. It is always wise to look for ways to improve the manner in which questions are constructed and asked.

Once the interview has been completed, the historian is likely to find it most helpful after it has been transcribed, particularly in typescript. Transcribing oral interviews is a time-consuming task, but it returns valuable results, despite the need to spend perhaps ten times or more the amount of time transcribing than it took to conduct the interview. When an interview has been transcribed it is eminently more useable. Indeed, the researcher can work through the pages of an interview far more quickly and efficiently than by rewinding and playing the tapes over and over again. If complete transcripts cannot be made, the researcher may chose to compile an index of key topics and dates for each tape. This index will prove worthwhile when it is time to begin the task of organizing one's notes and writing the history of the farm. The following guide should prove helpful for planning and conducting oral interviews:

Preparation

Make written and oral contact with your subject well in advance.
Let the respondent know about the subject and the parameters of the interview.
Make certain that you understand how to use the tape recorder.
Use tapes that last at least an hour on each side.
Take extra tapes and batteries.
Write down your questions.
Know something about the agricultural history of the area and the farm.

Techniques

Begin with family members.
Mix autobiographical and topical questions into the interview, all of which are designed to encourage recall and conversation and enhance the flow of the interview.
Have a clear understanding of the categories of questions, that is, topics and subtopics, in order to keep the respondents focused yet not inhibited. Remember you are asking the respondent to compress many decades or years of living and experience into 60 to 90 minutes (2 hours at the maximum) of reflection. The efficient use of time is essential.
Ask follow-up questions. With these questions you can probe for specific details and encourage even more expansive recall.
Do not prejudice the answer by indicating what you hope or expect to hear.

Be certain that the respondent has finished answering one question before you ask another. This can be exasperating if the interviewee habitually takes long pauses. Here, experience will be the best teacher.

Be certain that the setting is free of background noise that will interfere with the recording.

Interview only one person at a time, although exceptions to this rule may be necessary.

Remember that tact and sensitivity assist in dealing with most subjects.

Be persistent.

Try to get more than one interview about the same subject in order to provide different perspectives.

Evaluate the interview for the attitudes and values of the respondent as well as for factual accuracy.

Some farm historians engaged in oral history might want to use a video-camera. This interviewing technique, of course, is more expensive and obtrusive. Still, the historian may find it a valuable and challenging research tool.

The Interview

Locate the tape machine where it will clearly record the words but where it will not intimidate the respondent.

When the tape recorder starts, give the date, location, and the name of the interviewer as well as the name of the respondent. Set the respondent at ease, perhaps by playing back some preliminary social conversation so that the interviewee can hear the sound of his or her voice and, if need be, become more comfortable and less apprehensive about the tape recorder.

Remember that aggressive questioning may put the interviewee on the defensive, harm the rapport between the historian and the respondent, and place the interview in jeopardy. Start gently and build up to tough questions gradually.

Let the respondent do most of the talking.

Allow the interviewee to take the questions wherever he or she wants (within limits). Memory is imprecise and any question may provoke an answer to a question not asked.

Do not interrupt unless it is absolutely necessary to return the conversation to the matter at hand.

Write down follow-up questions along with names, dates, and unusual foreign words or phrases as well as physical nuances that are important to understanding the answer.

Ask only one question at a time.

Take written notes during the interview, especially if the respondent speaks softly or has a weak voice.

Try to get the respondent's written permission to use the interview in your history.

Do not hurry.

Be flexible.

Stop before the respondent is exhausted.

Afterward

Verify all points of fact, if possible.

When transcribing delete "verbal clutter," such as "you know," "er," "ah," and "uh-huh" as well as insignificant comments made by the interviewer that are used to keep the respondent talking through the answer to a question.

Remember, the less editing the better.

Whether you show the transcription to the respondent or not is a matter of professional debate. Some historians believe that if a respondent would like to see it, there is no harm in showing a transcription. They contend that if the historian plans to rely heavily on a particular interview when writing, it will be best to let the respondent see a transcription in order to correct matters of fact or emphasis. Others argue that the interview must remain unaltered and that the respondent does not have a right to see a transcription. Consequently, the farm historian will need to exercise his or her own judgment.

When the project is complete, do not erase the tapes. Keep them or donate them to your state historical society or nearby college or university library where they will provide a valuable research collection for generations.

ORAL HISTORY EXAMPLES

Oral histories of people related to the farm or people important to the agricultural history of the state or locale can provide detail, nuance, and color to your narrative that will be impossible to glean from other sources. The following three examples of oral history indicate the manner in which this research tool can be helpful to the farm historian. The first extract comes from an interview which the author conducted with Terry and Pat Schoenthaler, who are wheat farmers in

Kansas. The author conducted the second interview with Alfred M. Landon, who was governor of Kansas during the Dust Bowl years of the Great Depression as well as the Republican presidential nominee in 1936. It provides an important view, by a public figure, of agricultural problems that affected many farms in Kansas. The third example comes from a published interview conducted by historians employed by the Federal Writers' Project with former slaves in the 1930s.

SCHOENTHALER INTERVIEW
[July 20, 1995, Ellis, Kansas]

Hurt: Terry, how long have you been a farmer?

Terry: Since I have been about ten years old, I guess. I farmed with dad by choice some of the time, and also as a demand of parents as part of growing up, taking part of the workload. I left for about seven years to go to college at K-State. Then I taught school for a while and tried some other jobs, and then I guess I had an opportunity to go back to dad's farm. Dad had some health problems. So moved back to be a full-fledged farmer in 1976. Full-time farmer for nineteen years.

Hurt: Were your parents the first ones to own that farm?

Terry: No. Patty and I are the third generation on the farm now. My parents lived there, my grandfather bought the farm. The farm was the original homestead for the . . . where you plant trees [Timber Culture Act claim]. . . . My grandpa bought it from the original seller. You have to go back another generation to find that out.

Hurt: In the twenty years since you came back to the farm what are some of the most fundamental changes that you have seen on your farm?

Terry: Size would be the biggest thing. I remember when I was home as a kid . . . our wheat acreage was probably a fourth of what I'm presently farming, the crop size. Our cattle herd was only a third of what we have . . . everything is just getting bigger and larger.

Hurt: Do you have fewer neighbors then when you were a kid?

Terry: Definitely. Here you have to drive a couple miles further to find a neighbor now than you used to. I think that shows up in the school population here in town. . . . I used to ride a school bus, it was a fifty-passenger school bus. You could barely find a seat on it. When our kids rode the bus, it was the same sized bus, you'd be lucky to find twenty, twenty-five kids riding the bus.

Hurt: Given the problems or challenges of agriculture over the last twenty or thirty years, what do you have to deal with as a farm family today that you didn't have to deal with twenty years ago?

Pat: I think that women are probably getting much more involved in the farming. When we first moved back, well, the boys were very young and I didn't do very much except maybe run errands for Terry. But now I do most all of the field work, and I notice that with a lot of the neighbors it's that way. I guess twenty years ago mainly the women did the books . . . and run errands. Now I'll do just about everything. And I think the reason for that is you have so much money in your equipment and you want some one person that's always there. If you have your own investment in it you take real good care of it. . . . you can't find temporary help, you can't find teenagers that will work in the summer.

Terry: Our children spent a lot more time in town than I ever did.

Pat: They were involved in too many activities really. They didn't farm very much.

Terry: Weekends, that was about the only time I made it to town.

Hurt: What government programs are of most consequence to your farm today?

Pat: It's the deficiency payments.

Terry: The crop subsidies, especially for the wheat program.

Hurt: How has the marketing changed from the way your father marketed?

Terry: When you needed the money, you sold something. And they used to keep it for two or three years. This is what used to amaze me. Grandpa always had a bin of wheat that was from last year, just in case. Well this year, we got our harvest in, and we got to send some of it to meet the first note at the bank.

Hurt: What contact do you as a farmer and farm family have with extension agents today?

Terry: Here in Kansas we still have an extension office in every county. It is usually staffed with a minimum of two agents, usually an agent and a home economist. So, I can go to my county seat, and I have access to all the current publications plus the expertise. And, if I have a problem that he's not familiar with or needs more help on he can go to the area offices or to Manhattan to the state specialist.

Hurt: What social organizations have been important during the history of your farm?

Pat: Well we're Farm Bureau members, but the only reason we did that was for the health insurance and farm insurance type of thing. We don't go to actual Farm Bureau meetings or anything like that. We're just using it as a group to get a better price. . . .

Terry: I belong to a cattle association, a registered cattle association, register Gelviehs, a national organization. . . . We're members of the local cooperative. We're quite involved in that one as a board member and went to some national meetings.

Hurt: How is your livestock raising different from you dad?

Terry: I don't think my dad's cattle had weaning weights. They didn't have any production records at all. I have mine setup on the computer now. I can go back and they're indexed according to several different traits.

———————◄—

This brief example shows, in part, the importance of large-scale farming, rural depopulation, technological change, and the changing role of women on the farm. Oral interviews such as this are invaluable for writing the history of a farm. In this case, the participation of both Terry and Pat Schoenthaler worked well, because they complemented each other. Farm historians must let experience, logistics, and necessity be their guide concerning single or multiple participation in the interview.

LANDON INTERVIEW
[June 16, 1978, Topeka, Kansas]

Hurt: Governor Landon roughly forty years have passed since the black blizzards turned day into night on the southern plains. For those people who did not experience the Dust Bowl, it is hard for them to believe the dust storms were that bad. What are your recollections of the Dust Bowl?

Landon: Visibility on the streets in Topeka was down to half a mile in the dust storms. Men were losing their homes and their farms. Men were coming in with tears in their eyes, begging for jobs to save their farms or to send their boys or girls to college. It was just terrible. They [the dust storms] changed thousands of lives permanently.[1]

Hurt: As governor, what did you do to aid the drought-stricken people of the Dust Bowl?

Landon: I went back to see President Roosevelt [March, 1935] about the terrible changes in the lives of the people and [about] their losing their farms and homes. As a result of that, he sent M. L. Wilson out, and we started one morning and drove through Kansas. There were times you couldn't see past the radiator. As a result of that trip, one of their [federal government] recommendations was for government subsidies for farm ponds. You fly over Kansas [and] you see a lot of them. The state's covered with them.[2]

I appointed committees in every county on farm mortgage foreclosures to work out agreements with the banks or mortgage companies that they carry the loan. There were farm mortgage riots in every state adjoining Kansas. I had to work pretty [hard]. I took a hand in one or two—called the bank myself. I wouldn't say arm twisting. I remember I called one banker. I heard there was going to be a riot in [his] town. I talked to him about this fellow and [he] said, "We've carried him along, he makes no attempt to reciprocate, and he's just no good." So I said, "I'm not going to argue about that, but do you want a farm mortgage riot in your town tomorrow? If there is I'll have to send the troops in if the sheriff calls on me for this protection." I said, "You better ride along with the so and so a little longer anyhow. You've gone along with him for four or five years, another year or two won't make any difference."[3]

Hurt: During the 1950s, the drought and dust storms returned. How was the Dust Bowl different in the 1950s compared to the 1930s?

Landon: We've had high winds and we've had drought since then, but the technology is different. Big machinery breaks up the soil deeper. The deeper plowed, it doesn't blow. In 1933 it was still the horse. Horses instead of tractors. Tractors were just in the[ir] infancy in the early thirties. All farm machinery basically was still horse drawn and, of course, that's all changing now. You know the difference that makes [with] quicker cultivation and harvesting and so forth. So farming has changed; processes have changed as much in farming as they have in industry.

————————▶ ◀————————

Although Governor Landon's reminiscence is relatively clear, he was 90 years old at the time, and his answers tended to ramble. Consequently, some annotation is necessary to give his comments a necessary context. The historian, who conducts an oral history may need to incorporate the annotations in the form of foot- or endnotes to the narrative history of the farm. The three endnotes for the Landon interview are illustrative:

1. In spring, 1933, Landon received over 15,000 applications for 200 jobs that were available by gubernatorial appointment. See Donald R. McCoy, *Landon of Kansas* (Lincoln: University of Nebraska Press, 1966), 141. On March 22, 1935, Governor Landon sent a telegram concerning the wind erosion menace to Senator Arthur M. Capper. In that telegram Landon wrote: "It should be emphasized that this is not a Western Kansas problem alone. It involves an area embracing at least parts of the following states: Nebraska, Kansas, Oklahoma, New Mexico, and Colorado. We would still have dust menacing health conditions over the central western United States even though we checked our wind erosion in Kansas unless this problem is solved as a whole. It is too big for the individual county or one state alone to solve without assistance and the co-operation which can be obtained only through the federal government as the agency which steps in when you have all interstate problems. It will assist of course and make the work easier. The immediate emergency can be met only by listing and the planting of row crops. Again, let me emphasize that this is not the problem of a single state." Dust Bowl Scrapbook, Kansas State Historical Society.

2. In 1933, the legislature, upon Landon's request, provided an eighteen-month, real-estate redemption period to protect debtors against mortgage foreclosures. During the 1890s, Kansas Populists had provided similar legislation. In addition, with Landon's support, deficiency judgments were abolished for real estate foreclosures. See William Frank Zornow, *Kansas: A History of the Jayhawk State* (Norman: University of Oklahoma Press, 1961), 251–53.

3. Landon toured western Kansas in mid-April 1935, and called the Dust Bowl a "national catastrophe." He was adamant, however, that the region "never was a desert." See J. S. Ploughe, "Out of the Dust," *Christian Century* 52 (May 22, 1935): 691. M. L. Wilson served as the Assistant Secretary of Agriculture.

FEDERAL WRITERS' PROJECT INTERVIEW
[August 25, 1937, Timmonsville, South Carolina]

A third example of oral history comes from the Federal Writers' Project during the administration of Franklin Delano Roosevelt. Beginning in 1936, historians conducted a series of interviews with ex-slaves. These narratives were deposited in the Library of Congress, where typescript copies were prepared for publication. B. A. Botkin, Chief Editor, of the Writers' Unit of the Library of Congress said of these oral histories: "The narratives belong to folk history—history recovered from the memories and lips of participants or eye-witnesses, who mingle group with individual experience and both with observation, hearsay, and tradition. Whether the narrators relate what they actually saw and thought and felt, what they imagine, or what they have thought and felt about slavery since, now we know *why* they thought and felt as they did." These published oral histories can give the local historian in the South additional insights about the history of a farm or plantation, specifically or generally. Oral histories that have been collected by other people, whether published or not, are important sources for the local historian. Often such oral history collections are located at the state historical societies or in the manuscript collections of nearby college or university libraries.

The following oral history was taken by Lucille Young and R. Grady Davis. It is indicative of the value of oral testimony collected by others. Young and Davis conducted the interview with Jake McLeod, an 83-year-old ex-slave. The entire interview can be found in George P. Rawick (ed.), *The American Slave: A Composite Autobiography*, vol. 3, *South Carolina Narratives*, parts 3 and 4 (1941; Reprint, Westport, CT: Greenwood Press, 1971), 157–63. The reader does not know the questions asked, but the compiled responses provide important information about agriculture, labor, technology, nutrition, social life, literacy, and identity on a plantation.

> You see what color I am. I born in Lynchburg, South Carolina de 13th day of November, 1854. Born on de McLeod place. Grandparents born on de McLeod place too. . . .
>
> De McLeod, dey was good people. Believe in plenty work . . . but work us very reasonable. De overseer, he blow horn for us to go to work at sunrise. Give us tasks to do en if you didn't do it, dey put de little thing to you. Dat was a leather lash or some kind of whip. . . .
>
> My boss had four slave house dat was three or four hundred yards

from his house en I reckon he had about 25 slaves. One was pole house wid brick chimney en two rooms petitioned off en de other three was clay house. Us had frame bed en slept on shucks en hay mattresses. Dey didn't give us no money but had plenty to eat every day. Give us buttermilk en sweeten potatoes en meat en corn bread to eat mostly. . . . Den dey let us have a garden en extra patches of we own dat we work on Saturday evenings. . . .

I had to thin cotton en drop peas en corn en I was a half hand two years during de war. If a whole hand hoes one acre, den a half hand hoes half a acre. Dat what a half hand is. . . .

Wheat, peas, corn en cotton was de things dat peoples plant mostly in dem days. Dis how I see dem frail de wheat out. Put pole in hard land en drive horse in circle en let dem stamp it out. You could ride or walk. Two horses tramp en shake it out en den take straws en have somethin to catch it in en wind it out. Had to pick en trash a bushel of peas a day.

When corn haulin time come, every plantation haul corn en put in circle in front of de barn. Have two piles en point two captains. Dey take sides and give corn shuckin like dat. Shuck corn en throw in front of door en sometimes shuck corn all night. After they get through wid all de schuckin, give big supper en march all round old Massa's kitchen en house. Have tin pans, buckets en canes for music en dance in front of de house in de road. Go to another place en help dem shuck corn de next time en so on dat way. . . .

I don' remember freedom [Emancipation Day]. . . . We work on den for one third de crop de first year wid de boss furnishing everything. Soon as got little ahead went to sharecropping.

In this case, the interviewers chose to transcribe the oral account according to the manner in which Jake McLeod spoke. Had they edited it for correct grammar, sentence structure, and pronunciation, much of the character and context of the interview would have been lost. Most important, the transcription would have been inaccurate.

Conducting oral history, then, can be challenging and rewarding for the farm historian. The people who lived on the farm or who currently own or occupy it as well as those who have worked on the farm can provide information that cannot be gained from traditional written sources. In addition, oral history will help fill in the gaps of the written record, or, in some cases it may be the only record available. Like all research, however, oral history requires time and preparation. Yet, for anyone writing the history of a farm, oral history is likely to be essential.

SUGGESTED READINGS

A good introduction to oral history techniques can be found in David E. Kyvig and Myron A. Marty, *Nearby History: Exploring the Past around You* (Nashville: American Association for State and Local History, 1982). See also Patricia Pate Havlice, *Oral History: A Reference Guide and Annotated Bibliography* (Jefferson, NC: McFarland, 1985), and Eva M. McMahan and Kim Lacy Rogers, eds., *Interactive Oral History Interviewing* (Hillsdale, NJ: Erlbaum Associates, 1994). Other useful guides include Stephen Caunce, *Oral History and the Local Historian* (New York: Longman, 1994), Valerie Raleigh Yow, *Recording Oral History: A Practical Guide for Social Scientists* (Thousand Oaks, CA: Sage, 1994), Lee Smith, *Oral History* (New York: Putnam, 1983); and Jan Vansina, *Oral Tradition as History* (Madison: University of Wisconsin Press, 1985).

Anyone beginning an oral history project for the first time should also consult Ingrid Winther Scobie, "Family and Community History through Oral History," *Public Historian* 1 (Summer 1979): 29–39, and Paul Thompson, *The Voice of the Past: Oral History* (Oxford: Oxford University Press, 1978). Other introductory guides to the practice of oral history include Willa K. Baum, *Oral History for the Local Historical Society*, 3d ed., rev. (Nashville: American Association for State and Local History, 1987) as well as her study *Transcribing and Editing Oral History* (Nashville: American Association for State and Local History, 1977). See also James Hoopes, *Oral History: An Introduction for Students* (Chapel Hill: University of North Carolina Press, 1979); Barbara Allen and Lynwood Montell, *From Memory to History* (Nashville: American Association for State and Local History, 1981); and Linda Shopes, "Using Oral History for a Family History Project," American Association for State and Local History, *Technical Leaflet 123*, 1980. Two articles that show the importance of oral history as a research technique are James W. Lomax and Charles T. Morrissey, "The Interview as Inquiry for Psychiatrists and Oral Historians: Convergence and Divergence in Skills and Goals," *Public Historian* 11 (Winter 1989): 17–24; and Charles T. Morrissey, "The Two Sentence Format as an Interviewing Technique in Oral History Field Work," *Oral History Review* 15 (Spring 1987): 43–53.

More specialized guides include Jan Vansina, *Oral Tradition: A Study in Historical Methodology*, H. M. Wright, trans. (Chicago: Aldine Pub. Co., 1970). William L. Lang and Laurie K. Mercier, "Getting It Down Right: Oral History's Reliability in Local History Research," *Oral His-*

tory Review 12 (1984): 81–99; Barbara Allen, "Recreating the Past: The Narrator's Perspective in Oral History," *Oral History Review* 12 (1984): 1–12; Lewis Anthony Dexter, *Elite and Specialized Interviewing* (Evansville, IL: Northwestern University Press, 1970); Charles W. Joyner, "Oral History as Communicative Event: A Folkloristic Perspective," *Oral History Review* 7 (1979): 47–52; and E. Culpepper Clark, Michael J. Hyde, and Eva M. McMahan, "Communicating in the Oral History Interview: Investigating Problems of Interpreting Oral Data," *International Journal of Oral History* 1 (February 1980): 28–40.

For help on the use of a tape recorder and transcriptions see Edward D. Ives, *The Tape-Recorded Interview: A Manual for Workers in Folklore and Oral History* (Knoxville: University of Tennessee Press, 1980) and Cullom Davis, Kathryn Back, and Kay MacLean, *Oral history: From Tape to Type* (Chicago: American Library Association, 1977).

An excellent case study that shows how oral history can be used to write the history of a Mexican land grant in New Mexico is Charles L. Briggs, "Getting Both Sides of the Story: Oral History in Land Grant Research and Litigation," in *Land, Water, and Culture: New Perspectives on Hispanic Land Grants*, edited by Charles L. Briggs and John R. Van Ness (Albuquerque: University of New Mexico Press, 1987), 217–65.

All practioners of oral history can benefit from reading the works of Studs Terkel, particularly, *Hard Times: An Oral History of the Great Depression* (New York: Pantheon, 1970). Other suggested, specialized oral histories include Julie Jones-Eddy, *Homesteading Women: An Oral History of Colorado, 1890–1950* (New York: Twayne Publishers, 1992); Brett Harvey, *The Fifties: A Women's Oral History* (New York: Harper-Collins Pub., 1993); Ruth Edmonds Hill, (ed.), *The Black Women Oral History Project: From the Arthur and Elizabeth Schlesinger Library on the History of Women in America* (Westport, CT: Meckler, 1991); and *Oral History Stories of the Long Walk + Hweeldi Baa Hane* (Crownpoint, NM: Lake Valley Navajo School, 1991).

Chapter 4

PHOTOGRAPHS, MAPS, AND ARTIFACTS

Historians will find photographs, maps, and artifacts particularly useful for studying the history of a farm. Each provides documentary evidence; only the form is different from written records. Usually, the photographs will be in a personal collection or in the possession of family, relatives, or friends. People who are not nearby can be written to, told of the project, and asked about both general and specific photographs of the farm. If a farm belonged to an important family or a corporation, the local library, county historical society, or state historical society may have photographs. The local newspaper may also have a photo morgue or archives available for public research. Or, if the corporation is still in operation, photographs might be on file in its archives or public relations office.

Photographs are important documentary evidence for the history of a farm, because each freezes a moment of the past. If the photographs are properly handled, the moment is preserved for all time. Photographs can show important events on the farm, for example, the raising of a new barn, a prize 4-H calf and its owner, the family kitchen, or garden. Photographs help the historian understand matters of time and place, such as the autumn harvest during the 1890s on an Ohio farm. They also aid in the study of the details of a farm's history; the new Farmall tractor purchased in 1924, the crew of Mexican men, women, and children at work in a California lettuce field, or the Connecticut family harvesting tobacco at the turn of the twentieth century. Studying the people, their arrangement, and clothing as well as physical features—buildings, equipment, livestock, and social relationships—can assist one to understand the nature of farm life at that moment.

Photographs, like written documents, must be read and analyzed to understand their meaning and aid historical research. In order to do so, the farm historian needs to learn to ask the right questions. The first question will be an intuitive: "What is pictured?" Then, more specifically: "What is the setting?" "Where was the photograph taken?" "When was the photograph taken?" "Who are the people?" "What is the context of the photograph?" "What does it tell us?" "What does it mean to the history of the farm?" Perhaps the photograph identifies owners or tenants of the farm, shows labor and cropping patterns, architecture, farmyard layout, or implements as well as domestic chores or social activities. The historian ought to think about what is shown and excluded as well as the arrangement or composition of the photograph. The photograph shows what the photographer considered to be important, that is, what he or she wanted to remember. Consequently, the historian is wise not only to look at the subject matter but also to analyze the motive of the photographer and the nature of the time and circumstance in which it was taken.

Photographs are important because they not only provide general information about a subject or event, but they also enable the historian to study the past for details that easily are overlooked, forgotten, considered of no consequence, or even omitted from written records. Carefully studied photographs can enable greater understanding of the life, times, and culture of people who lived on a farm at a given moment and about the physical features of the farm, such as the land, fields, and buildings, than are provided by written records. Indeed, pictures can indicate a great deal about farm work, social class, standard of living, and valuation of the farm.

The historian must be cautious, however, and question the authenticity of photographs. It is not particularly important that photographs were staged with people posing uncomfortably and formally, but it is important to recognize a fake, such as the one shown below. During the 1930s, a portion of the southern Great Plains became known as the Dust Bowl, because drought, wind erosion, and careless agricultural practices helped cause dust storms that turned day into night, ruined the land, and took human lives. This photo shows a horde of jack rabbits fleeing in terror before an oncoming "black blizzard." It is, of course, a fake. The line through the center of that photograph attests to the joining of two images that have been reproduced as one. Dust storms blew across the land with great savagery and the rabbit population exploded during the drought years, but this scene never occurred. Farm historians should eagerly seek photographs to aid their work, but they must always give those sources as much critical analysis as they would any written document.

Photographs can be important documents for research, but the local historian must guard against fakes such as this composite. *Kansas State Historical Society.*

The barn photograph shown below was taken about the turn of the twentieth century. Based on the barn's architecture, the clothing style of the people, and a cryptic note on the back of the picture, the photographer probably took it in northeastern Ohio. More precisely, however, it tells the historian a great deal about the division of labor, when the men were responsible for the heavy lifting, while the women (on the left) prepared the food for on-site meals. The photograph also confirms that neighbors shared their labor and that barn raising also served as a social experience.

Similarly, threshing time was a social occasion as well as hard work. Steam engines and threshing machines were expensive and most farmers could not afford them. Instead, they often hired a threshing crew. In this photograph, the owner of the steam engine stands on the platform at the rear, while his workers, perhaps sons and neighbors, operate the threshing machine. This photograph also provides a good look at the operation of a steam engine and threshing machine in Missouri during the early twentieth century.

Domestic scenes in the farmyard or inside the home also help the historian trace the history of a farm. In 1919, the Virginia farm woman shown below ironed in her kitchen. Notice the wood-burning stove on the left with another iron heating. This photograph tells much about farm life and the standard of living in this home before it was wired for electricity. Now, compare it with the photograph of the farm

This barn building photograph tells much about architectural, labor, and social history in rural Ohio during the late nineteenth century. The local historian often will find that a magnifying glass helps study the details in historical photographs. *Courtesy of the Ohio Historical Society.*

Agricultural photographs can help the local historian learn much about farming practices. This photo shows the threshing process before the farmer cut his wheat with a combine. *Courtesy of the Massie, Natural Resources Division, State Historical Society of Missouri, Columbia.*

woman who is working in her kitchen approximately thirty years later. What changes can be identified?

Similarly, the photograph of homesteaders posing before their sod house during the 1890s shows not only their most prized possessions—a horse and table—but also a sturdy home with a wooden door and roof (covered with sod) and a glass window (a sure sign of success as well as providing access to the world beyond). As such, it tells a great deal about their economic situation as they posed in their best clothes.

Not all photographs will be historically significant, and the historian always ought to ask whether the image tells anything useful about the farm. Photographs are valuable to the historian, of course, only to the extent that they can be identified and interpreted. If photographs have not been identified on the back, the historian can seek verification by asking those who might know about it. People, buildings, or natural features may be identified by friends, relatives, acquaintances, or other photographs. Careful scholars do not settle for

Photographs of the farm home help the historian evaluate daily chores, personal relationships, layout of work space, and standards of living. *Courtesy of Library of Congress.*

guess work. If the photograph cannot be identified or reasonably dated, it is better left unused as a research document.

Photographs should be used as illustrative material in a history, only if the images supplement the narrative. Pictures should not be included merely for window dressing. Photographs illustrate a manuscript more effectively when captions are provided. Captions enable the historian to include information that does not easily fit elsewhere in the text. Consequently, the best captions are often those that run for two or three sentences. A caption of only a few words, such as "Dairy barn, 1924," is better than nothing, but more helpful would be, for example, "Adam Story built this dairy barn in 1924. It was based on a round design that specialists touted as being more efficient than other designs. This barn set the precedent for the building of other round barns in Black Hawk County, Iowa." Extremely long captions, however, may become tedious to read. The key is to tell something meaningful about the photograph that will strengthen the history of the

During the 1930s electricity dramatically changed the lives of many farm families. Refrigerators replaced iceboxes and eliminated the winter task of cutting ice or the need to purchase it, while improving food preservation. *Courtesy of the United States Department of Agriculture.*

farm, while at the same time allowing the picture to do most of the work of providing a glimpse of the past that is both interesting and informative.

If one is going to publish a history along with pictures it is best to use continuous-tone photographs, that is, the original picture or a copy developed from a negative. Unless absolutely necessary, it is wise not to use photographs that have been published in a book or magazine. These photographs are called half-tones. This means that they have been screened, that is, broken into a series of dots by the printer in order to be reproduced in the publication. A printer necessarily will screen a half-tone again. When the image is printed the second time, it will have more dots and a fuzzy, muddy, undefined look.

Occasionally, an illustration that shows a piece of machinery used on the farm comes not from a continuous-tone photograph, but rather a drawing from a trade catalog or advertisement. In this case, the im-

Family photographs taken at any stage of the farm's history can tell the local historian a great deal about the origin and development of a farm. Photographs that show change over time will help trace that history in a manner that written documents cannot match. This photograph was taken in Finney County, Kansas, about 1890. *Kansas State Historical Society.*

These migrant agricultural workers endured tiresome stoop labor in a spinach field on a large-scale truck farm in California during the 1930s. *Courtesy of the California State Library, Sacramento, California.*

age can be copied either as a continuous-tone photograph or as line art. The continuous-tone photo will have a gray background in place of the white page. Sometimes this background may be desirable. On other occasions one only wants the image. If so, the image can be photographed as line art by using color film. It will capture only the black lines of the print, and it will leave the background white.

Cotton picking time brought sharecroppers, tenants, and agricultural laborers into the fields every autumn before the mechanization of crop harvesting during the mid-twentieth century. *Courtesy Georgia Department of Archives and History.*

Agricultural labor varied across the nation prior to the age of widespread mechanization. In the state of Washington these workers picked apples about the turn of the twentieth century. *Courtesy of the Washington State Historical Society, Tacoma.*

In using historical photographs from an album it is a good idea to make sure that the images have the best exposure possible, if one has a choice. Over-exposed or under-exposed images will not reproduce satisfactorily. Moreover, one is wise to choose the photograph with the greatest clarity. If photographs are not of first-class quality, they

Before the adoption of combines, farmers used binders to cut small grains, such as wheat and oats. The bound sheaves, however, had to be placed in shocks to help cure the grain before pickup for threshing. *Courtesy of the Washington State Historical Society, Tacoma.*

should probably be left out of a publication. If a history will remain in typescript or photocopy form, greater leeway exists with the quality of images used. If a history is photocopied for distribution among family members, copies of the best photographs may well be included. Although photocopied pictures usually have limited value, they can enhance a history for family distribution when appropriately placed throughout the text. However, if photographs are uniformly bad, they should not be used for illustrations. Rather, they should be used for evidence and to help craft a narrative.

Occasionally, photographs are too brittle, torn, or glued down to use. In this case, they should be copied. A professional photographer easily can do this copy work. To save money this can be done with a 35 millimeter single-lens, reflex camera. Doing so requires a copy stand, lights, and a "macro" lens. These three items will allow proper focus on the photograph. A piece of nonglare glass placed over the image will keep the photo flat during the copying process and will not reflect the glare of the lighting.

Given this introduction to the use of photographs as historical documents, study the four photographs of farmworkers shown below. What can you tell about the farms, in the broadest context, where these photographs were taken?

POSTERS

Posters, also called broadsides, can tell much about a farm. The poster shown below indicates that Tenwick W. Dunlop and Dennis H. Driesbach were large-scale and successful breeders of purebred Duroc hogs. Their business was large enough not only to merit a sale conducted by two auctioneers, but also to have a printed catalog for prospective customers. In addition, they offered convenient delivery by a nearby railroad.

MAPS

Topographical maps are useful for gaining an overview of the physical lay of the farm's land. They will show hills, valleys, rivers, creeks—all of which will help the historian learn why certain things were done on the farm in specific locations, or why certain things were not done. These maps enable the historian to gain an understanding of special relationships by giving a bird's-eye view of the farm. These

Farmers who offered specialized services, such as the breeding of purebred live-stock, often advertised in the local newspapers and distributed flyers and posters to announce special sales. *Author's Collection.*

maps can be obtained for virtually any area in the United States either from the U.S. Geological Survey or state geological survey offices. Often these state agencies have deposited their geological survey maps with the state historical society. These collections usually are little used, but they merit the attention of all historians, particularly the farm historian.

County atlases usually contain a plat or map for each township. These maps will also show property lines and the names of the landowners as well as the location of roads, railroads, and towns. It is quite possible to find a farm on a plat map in a county atlas. This map will likely provide an idealized look of the farm, but it will nevertheless help the historian understand the layout, architecture, and daily activities at that particular time. At the very least, these old county atlases will enable farm historians to gain a better understanding of the county's agricultural practices, markets, and related affairs. Still, these histories primarily emphasized local elites. Most farmers and their farms were not included because they could not or would not pay the monetary price to do so.

MARKS AND BRANDS REGISTRIES

Since the eighteenth century, if not before, counties registered earmarks and brands. The county clerk kept these records. A county still may have an active roll. These registries contained the date, name, and description of the earmark or brand of the farm or ranch. These marks and brands helped farmers identify wandering or lost livestock, particularly hogs and cattle. These books sometimes had a drawing of the particularly mark or brand alongside the written description. If the researcher knows the names of the people who owned or lived on the farm at a particular time, he or she might be able to locate the proper earmark or brand used to identify the hogs and cattle of the farm or ranch.

ARTIFACTS

Tracing the technological history of a farm can be both fascinating and hard work. In either case, it can be a great deal of fun. The place to begin is in the barn, tool or machine shed, or graveyard for discarded implements located somewhere on the farm. Working through the barn and machine shed allows one to see what kinds of implements are being used today. Then looking in the corners, walls, and out-of-the-way places may reveal agricultural equipment and tools no longer in use. The next step is to examine carefully the implements that have been junked long ago behind the barn, granary, or in some other unseen, isolated part of the farm. It is wise to list everything seen and make notes about the tools and implements that cannot be identified. The owner or tenant can be asked about these implements. Perhaps the owner or operator will show off the premises and identify

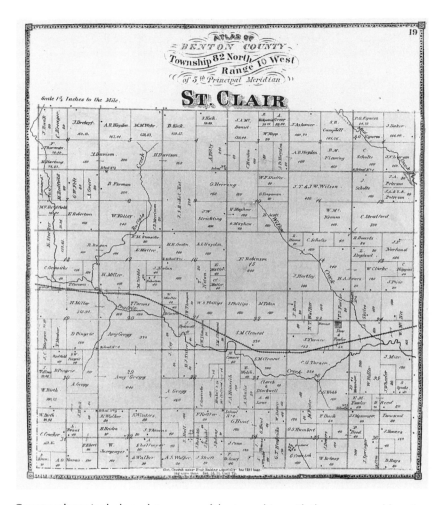

County atlases include a plat or map of the township, with the names and location of the farm families. This map shows the location of farmers in an Iowa township in 1872. *Author's Collection.*

equipment in the process. Family members and neighbors may be able to help. If a particular piece of equipment baffles everyone, it is a good idea to take pictures of it from different angles or make detailed sketches. This will help the identification process from trade catalogs or other photographs at a library or state historical society.

The easiest way to trace the technological history of a farm is to

BAYLOR COUNTY

PAIR OF SPURS
G. F. Boone
Seymour, Texas

BRIDLE BIT
S. A. Clark
Seymour, Texas

7H HALF CIRCLE
Bud Holt
Seymour, Texas

PAIR OF BOOTS
H. R. Martin
Comanche, Texas

KEY NO
Cablero Mathis
Seymour, Texas

3 BLOCKS
W. H. Portwood
Seymour, Texas

ANCHOR
W. F. Robertson
Seymour, Texas

HASH KNIFE
E. C. Sterling & Sons
Seymour, Texas

DOUBLE ANCHOR
Lou Stout
Bomarton, Texas

SCISSORS
R. A. Talley & Co.
Seymour, Texas

A HORN
R. W. Talley
Seymour, Texas

C LAZY T
Carter Taylor
Seymour, Texas

BEXAR COUNTY

RECTANGLE LAZY R
J. A. Ackerman
San Antonio, Texas

CA CONNECTED
A. J. Cichon
San Antonio, Texas

IOU
Ruth P. Davidson
San Antonio, Texas

HALF CIRCLE LONG D
Michael Delany
San Antonio, Texas

INVERTED 2 DJ
Juan Delgads
San Antonio, Texas

RAFTER DOT
J. M. Dobie
San Antonio, Texas

DOLLAR MARK
Ernest Eastwood
San Antonio, Texas

LAZY ANCHOR
M. B. Farin
San Antonio, Texas

RF CONNECTED
Alfred Friesenbohm
San Antonio, Texas

RECTANGLE L
J. M. Hawkins
San Antonio, Texas

CIRCLE ARROW
J. L. Hensley
San Antonio, Texas

LAZY LR
Leon Ramzinski
San Antonio, Texas

R DOWN & UP HALF CIRCLE
Rosa Reisinger
San Antonio, Texas

BR CONNECTED
Benito Rodriquez
San Antonio, Texas

SNAKE S
Albert Schmitt
San Antonio, Texas

WA CONNECTED
George Washington
San Antonio, Texas

S LAZY T
Charles Weir
San Antonio, Texas

LAZY B
Bud Wood
San Antonio, Texas

Ranchers registered these brands in Baylor and Bexar counties in Texas during the nineteenth century. In other locales, the country clerk also registered earmarks for hogs. *Author's Collection.*

work backward, identifying the most recent forms of technology and progressing to the earliest. This procedure enables one to deal with the artifacts of the past—three-dimensional objects—that can be as useful in research as manuscript and printed sources. Even though artifacts are tangible evidence of the past, the historian must be careful to correctly identify items, learn about how they worked, and establish their significance in American agriculture. Then, the historian will be able to assess the importance of this technology to the history of the farm.

An inventory of the current technology of the farm will be useful. This inventory should be divided into time periods, such as 1950–present, 1900–1950, 1850–1900, and 1800–1850. These dates are fairly arbitrary and the technological development in one period overlaps its successor. Even so, by being able to identify tools and implements by rough chronological periods, the historian can achieve a better understanding of sequential development, and cause and effect. The assignment of more precise dating can come later.

Besides assigning chronological categories, the historian also would do well to categorize particular implements by function. Six broad groups will serve most needs:

1. Tillage equipment, such as plows, disks, chisels, listers, harrows, and spades, that prepare the fields for crops.
2. Planting implements, such as grain drills, planters, broadcast seeders (both hand- and horse-powered), that place seeds or small plants in the soil.
3. Cultivation implements that cut off and kill the weeds and which loosen the soil to aid moisture penetration, soil conservation, and aeration, such as double-shovel plows, sulky cultivators, and horse- and tractor-drawn cultivators.
4. Harvesting implements that are designed for specific crops, such as reapers, wheat and corn binders, corn shockers, cotton harvesters, combines, threshing machines, husker-shredders, mowers, cranberry rakes, sickles, scythes, and flails.
5. Livestock equipment, such as milking machines, separators, curd cutters, cheese presses, horse or mule collars, dehorners, harnesses, branding irons, saddles, and bits.
6. Miscellaneous implements and tools necessary for farming over time that do not fit in the major categories, such as windmills, wagons, manure spreaders, ditching plows, axes, adzes, and various unidentifiable items.

Once a basic inventory has been made, it is now time to determine how the implement worked, and who made it and when. An overview of technological change can be gained from the suggested readings at the end of this chapter. These books not only provide many pictures and illustrations but also information about manufacturing, and the significance of many forms of agricultural technology. Old agricultural magazines at a nearby library or historical society may help as well as Sears and Roebuck and Montgomery Ward catalogs. Trade catalogs also deserve a look. Late nineteenth- and early twentieth-century trade catalogs were published by implement companies for advertising and selling purposes. These catalogs usually provide an illustration or photograph of the implement, such as a mower or reaper, and a brief description about its workings, capacity, and often a price list for the implement and spare parts. Patent numbers, company names, and the color of paint will also enable precise identification of such implements as the Buckeye self-rake reaper, Miller mower, or Huber steam engine. Trade catalogs, then, will help distinguish implements as well as explain their significance to the farm either in terms of acceptance or later rejection.

Careful observation of an implement's design and comparison of it to illustrations and photographs in archival collections, trade catalogs, or equipment and tool encyclopedias are essential research techniques. Other physical evidence is also important. Well-worn handles on a plow, for example, indicate long, hard use, a sure sign that the implement played a significant role in the history of the farm.

Although many agricultural implement companies have gone out of business, the researcher can use the annual *Supplement and Tractor Product File* (Kansas City, MO: Intertec Pub., Corp.) for current addresses of farm equipment manufacturers. The *Report of the Federal Trade Commission on the Manufacture and Distribution of Farm Implements* (Washington, DC: Government Printing Office, 1948) will help the historian trace company mergers. In trying to identify and date a piece of equipment for which the company is in operation, the archivist and the director of public relations at the company headquarters can often provide help based on their files of old trade catalogs, specifications, and patents. It is wise to send along as much identifying material as possible, including a photograph. Owners' manuals, advertisements, and back issues of *Iron Men Album* and *Gas Engine Magazine* can also help the historian identify and date farm equipment, especially steam engines and gasoline tractors.

The workings of various implements often is best understood by

RUSSELL TRACTION ENGINE
SIX, TEN, THIRTEEN AND SIXTEEN HORSE

Trade catalogs will help the local historian identify implements used on the farm. This drawing shows a Russell steam traction engine that became popular among farmers who could afford them during the late nineteenth century. Trade catalogs will provide specific names and model numbers and often tell something about the operation of the implement. *Author's Collection.*

asking someone who used them or who used similar equipment, such as a horse-drawn corn planter, grain binder, or steam engine. This research offers an excellent opportunity for oral history. If oral history is not possible, communication by letter also may be helpful. Photographs or photocopies and descriptions of the implement will assist a correspondent. Be prepared to ask questions. If someone calls a particular sulky plow a horse killer, ask why?

The skillful farm historian studies implements carefully. Farmers are very utilitarian and thrifty. They may have used the handles, wheels, shovels, or seat from one implement to repair another implement. Unmatched paint is a sign that parts of the implement are not original. Trademarks, names, parts, and patent numbers also may help determine whether a particular implement has cannibalized parts on it. Usually, however, these problems will not prevent the historian from identifying most of the implements on a farm and determining their significance.

Newspapers published during the nineteenth century also may help the historian determine the kinds of agricultural technology

This farmer is using a Model GP John Deere tractor with a corn picker in 1928. Company archivists sometimes can help identify farm implements. *Courtesy of the Deere and Company Archives.*

used in a local area. Newspapers often advertised implements for which licenses could be purchased in order for local entrepreneurs to make and sell these implements. Newspapers enable the historian to see the kinds of implements that could be purchased from local merchants or ordered from agents in major cities if transportation was available, such as a river, railroad, or major roadway. These advertisements, of course, do not in any way imply that this technology was used on the farm under study, but they will give the historian an idea of the kinds of implements available to farmers.

The historian also is likely to find inventories for taxes, estate sales, or personal account books invaluable. Each provides an accurate identification of the agricultural implements available at a particular time, and the value or cost of each. Still, such lists do not guarantee that these implements were used at that time. Inventories may be just that—cumulative lists. Even so, records such as these provide crucial

Newspapers can be helpful for the identification of the technology used on the farm at various times. This advertisement for a corn sheller appeared in a Philadelphia newspaper in 1817. *Author's Collection.*

information by showing the number, value, and kinds of implements used on a farm. By studying these records, the historian can gain an indication of the types of work conducted, scale of operation, and the amount of investment that the farm family made in tools and equipment. The following extrapolation from a probate record is indicative of the type of information that can be gleaned from these sources. This information was compiled by the appraisers for the estate of John Locke Hardeman, a large-scale farmer in Saline County, Missouri, on August 4, 1858. The appraisers listed every item of property and assessed its value. A selection from Hardeman's probate inventory shows some of his farm implements and their valuation:

1 ox wagon & bed	$ 40.00
1 4-horse wagon and bed	60.00
1 4-horse wagon and bed	70.00
1 2-horse wagon and harness	50.00
1 McCormick mower & reaper	70.00
1 old hemp brake	50.00
1 prairie plow	3.00
1 patent hemp brake & wagon	550.00
1 McCormick reaper hemp attachment	200.00
1 hemp break	7.50
1 corn miller	5.00
1 one old grist mill & horse power	40.00
1 thresher	25.00
1 wheat fan	15.00
12 1-horse plows	48.00
1 cultivator	16.00
3 hay forks	1.50
5 grubbing hoes	5.00
1 straw cutter	15.00
2 harrows	20.00
1 2-horse plow	27.00
5 mowing blades	9.00
4 wheat cradles	12.00
6 hemp cradles	24.00

Sometimes the farm historian may not be able to identify a particular piece of equipment. If a patent number can be located on it, however, the historian can write to the Patent Office in Crystal City, Maryland, and receive a copy of the patent specification papers. These papers provide a description of the implement and a drawing. Patent specification numbers, inventors, and patent drawings also can be found and cross-checked in the *Annual Report of the Commissioner of Patents to Congress*. This source includes an index. Moreover, if someone associated with the farm is known to have patented agricultural implements, these reports will provide the date of patent, the name of the implement, its description, and often a drawing of it.

Patent specification papers or patents do not mean that a particular implement was made and sold. In fact, this documentation merely means that the inventor developed something unique and received governmental protection for its production and sale so that others could not reproduce that invention for their own use or profit without paying for it. Frequently, agricultural patents involve little more than nuts and bolts adjustments or changes that allegedly made the plow, reaper, or cultivator different from all of the other products. Patents can be confusing rather than illuminating, probably because inventors often are not good technical writers. In these cases, researchers are obliged to work through the prose to the best of their ability to determine how the implement worked.

The use of photographs, maps, and artifacts as research sources can be exciting and rewarding, but, their use and interpretation require skill and careful analysis. Each will provide answers that cannot be gained from written documents, and each can supply helpful information for writing the history of a farm.

SUGGESTED READINGS

The best introduction to the use of photographs, maps, and artifacts remains David E. Kyvig and Myron A. Marty, *Nearby History: Exploring the Past around You* (Nashville: American Association for State and Local History, 1982) and Thomas Schlereth, *Artifacts of the American Past* (Nashville: American Association for State and Local History, 1980). See also Ian M. Quimby, ed., *Material Culture and the Study of American Life* (New York: Norton, 1978); Thomas Schlereth, *Material Culture Studies in America* (Nashville: American Association for State and Local History, 1980); Patrick H. Butler, III, *Material Culture as a Resource in Local History* (Chicago: Newberry Library, 1979); and John Chavis, "The Artifact and the Study of History," *Curator* 7 (June 1964): 156–62. For an excellent introduction to documentary agricultural photography see F. Jack Hurley, *Portrait of a Decade: Roy Stryker and the Development of Documentary Photography in the Thirties* (Baton Rouge: Louisiana State University Press, 1972).

For more specific information concerning the use of photographs in historical research see Jonathan Bayer, *Reading Photographs: Understanding the Aesthetics of Photography* (New York: Pantheon, 1977); James T. Booke, *A Viewer's Guide to Looking at Photographs* (Wilmette, IL: Aurelia, 1977); and Thomas L. Davies, *Shoots: A Guide to Your Family's Photographic Heritage* (Danbury, NH: Addison House, 1977). Although the study concerns urban photographs, the historian of a farm can learn much from Glen E. Holt, "Chicago through a Camera Lens: An Essay on Photography as History," *Chicago History* 1, no. 3 (1971): 158–69.

Researchers who have worked through the above literature may find more scholarly studies useful, such as Howard Becker, "Photography and Sociology," *Studies in the Anthropology of Visual Communications* 1 (Fall 1974): 3–26; John Collier, *Visual Anthropology: Photography as a Research Method* (New York: Rinehart and Winston, 1967); and Jon Wagner, ed., *Images of Information: Still Photography in the Social Sciences* (Beverley Hills, CA: Sage, 1979). For help choosing camera lenses for your own documentary photographic work see Gary Gore, "Zooming in on History: Basic Camera Lenses," *History News* 35 (September 1980): 44–45.

Research on maps should begin at the state historical society or in the map collection of a nearby college or university. Several good guides include James C. Wheat and Christian F. Brun, *Maps and Charts Published in America before 1800: A Bibliography* (New Haven: Yale University Press, 1969); Clara E. LeGear, *United States Atlases: A List of National, State, County, City, and Regional Atlases in the Library of Congress*, 2 vols. (Washington, DC: Library of Congress, 1950–1953); and Ralph E. Ehrenberg, *Geographical Exploration and Mapping in the Nineteenth Century: A Survey of the Records in the National Archives*, National Archives, *Research Information Paper No. 66* (Washington, DC: National Archives, 1973). See also Norman J. W. Thrower, "The County Atlas of the United States," *Surveying and Mapping* 21 (September 1961): 365–73.

R. Douglas Hurt, *American Farm Tools: From Hand Power to Steam Power* (Manhattan, KS: Sunflower Press, 1982) provides an illustrated history of nineteenth-century farm equipment that will aid with identification. This book covers tillage, seeding, harvesting, threshing, and hay and fodder making implements as well as steam engines. A companion reference that will help with the identification of gasoline tractors can also be found in R. Douglas Hurt, *Agricultural Technology in the Twentieth Century* (Manhattan, KS: Sunflower Press, 1991). See also P. L. Ardrey, *American Agricultural Implements* (Chicago: The Author, 1894); Leo Rogin, *The Introduction of Farm Machinery in Its Relation to the Productivity of Labor in Agriculture of the United States During the Nineteenth Century* (Berkeley: University of California Press, 1931);

and Robert C. Williams, "Antique Farm Equipment," American Association for State and Local History, *Technical Leaflet 101*, 1977. A good illustrated history of harvesting implements is Graeme R. Quick and Wesley F. Buchele, *The Grain Harvesters* (St. Joseph, MI: American Society of Agricultural Engineers, 1978).

Two excellent guides to the identification of steam engines are Floyd Clymer, *Album of Historical Steam Traction Engines and Threshing Equipment* (Los Angeles: The Author, 1949), and Jack Norbeck, *Encyclopedia of American Steam Traction Engines* (Sarasota, FL: Crestline Pub., 1976). The best history of the development and adoption of steam traction engines is Reginald M. Wik, *Steam Power on the American Farm* (Philadelphia: University of Pennsylvania Press, 1953). Two excellent sources for the identification of gasoline tractors are R. B. Gray, *The Agricultural Tractor, 1855–1950* (St. Joseph, MI: American Society of Agricultural Engineers, 1975), and C. H. Wendel, *Encyclopedia of American Farm Tractors* (Sarasota, FL: Crestline Pub., 1975). Researchers will also find Wendel's, *150 Years of International Harvester* (Sarasota, FL: Crestline Pub., 1981) useful for the identification of IHC tractors and implements.

A good general introduction to the history of American agricultural technology is John T. Schlebecker, *Whereby We Thrive: A History of American Farming, 1607–1972* (Ames: Iowa State University Press, 1975). For a more detailed study of the importance of technological change on the farm see Wayne D. Rasmussen, "The Impact of Technological Change on American Agriculture, 1862–1962," *Journal of Economic History* 22 (December 1962): 578–91. The best source for the identification of windmills is T. Lindsay Baker, *A Field Guide to American Windmills* (Norman: University of Oklahoma Press, 1985). See also, R. Douglas Hurt, "Wind Catchers and Eye Catchers: Technology Down on the Farm," *Timeline* 2 (April–May 1985): 26–39.

For an illustrated and descriptive introduction to hand tools found in many eighteenth- and nineteenth-century farm tool sheds, especially in the northern United States, see Eric Sloan, *A Museum of Early American Farm Tools* (New York: Funk and Wagnalls, 1964). See also Louis M. Roehl, *Harness Repairing* (Milwaukee: Bruce Pub. Co., 1921); *The Harness Maker and His Tools* (N.P.: San Joaquin County Historical Museum, 1976); and Louis Taylor, *Bits: Their History, Use and Misuse* (New York: Harper & Row, 1966).

Chapter 5

FARM LIFE

The history of a farm involves more than telling the story of land acquisition, technological change, architectural styles, and crop and livestock production. It also calls for the reconstruction of daily life in its social context. The historian may learn much by asking about the local, state, and national organizations joined by families who have lived on the farm. The researcher may also profit from examining the manner in which religious activities, education, mail service, automobiles, electricity, radios, telephones, and televisions as well as births and inheritance affected farm life. In order to give life and vibrancy to the history of a farm as well as cast it the broadest possible scope to determine its significance, the social story is invaluable.

The social history of the farm draws on all of the research techniques that have been discussed. While it is rare to be able to detail every aspect of daily life on the farm, the researcher will profit from being as thorough as possible. A few details may enable the historian to make generalizations that bridge the gap between the known and the unknown without going beyond the evidence. If one research technique fails to provide the answer to a question, the historian can shift to another methodology. If, for example, the written records do not tell when the owner or tenant of the farm joined the Farm Bureau or acquired telephone service, oral history might reveal the answers.

ORGANIZATIONS

Given the land acquisition patterns in the United States, farmers have lived outside the confines of towns and villages in contrast to the European tradition. By so doing, they have been isolated from community life, at least until road construction and automobiles improved transportation. Although the breakdown of rural isolation differed among regions, many farm families had to cope with being alone well into the twentieth century. When they had the opportunity for social interaction, however, most farm families took advantage of it. As a result, historians can learn much about the history of farms, if they can identify the social organizations that have been important to the families who have lived on the farm over time.

During the late nineteenth century, for example, the Patrons of Husbandry, commonly known as the Grange, became a popular organization for farmers. First established by Oliver Hudson Kelley in 1867 as a social and educational organization to help end rural isolation, it also became important to the cooperative movement during the late nineteenth century. The members organized local and state granges that affiliated with the national association. On the local level, the Grange sponsored lectures on improved agricultural techniques, circulated magazines and newspapers, and held picnics for the purpose of improving knowledge about the outside world and encouraging social interaction.

In order to investigate membership in an organization, such as the Grange, the researcher should check the pertinent letters, diaries, and newspaper scrapbooks and ask the farm operators whether they have been or are members of the organization. If these sources do not provide all of the information that is needed, a trip to the state historical society and to the local library will be necessary. The manuscript collections at the state historical society often include collections relating to the Grange and other agricultural organizations in that particular state. These records will contain membership lists, if they were saved, and documentation concerning the affairs of the organization.

In addition to manuscript collections, organizations often published annual proceedings. The local library should be able to acquire those sources through interlibrary loan. For example, the Grange publishes an annual volume called *Journal of Proceedings of the National Grange of the Patrons of Husbandry*. It provides an overview of the main concerns of the organization and, until well into the twentieth century, it included state summaries. These summaries give important information about membership, expenditures, and affairs. The following example comes from the report from California in the *Proceedings* for 1884, and it is representative of the information that the historian can gain from this source:

> This has been a hard year for California farmers, yet the interest in the Grange is not diminished, but continually growing stronger. We

have a number of business houses that are doing a thriving business. Among the number especially noticeable are the "Grangers' business Association," of San Francisco, and also of Sacramento; the "Farmers' Union," of Stockton and San Jose, and the "Grangers' Bank," of San Francisco. There are also a large number of smaller houses located in the northern and central sections of the state, doing a large amount of business, owned and controlled exclusively by Patrons of Husbandry.

The *California Patron*, the organ of our Order in the State, is in a prosperous condition. . . .

Number of Granges in California is 54, and the paying membership is 2,863.

From this extract, the farm historian learns the name of the state Grange newspaper, the cooperative businesses that the patrons operated and their locations, the number of granges, and the total membership. Other agricultural organizations provide similar information. The historian is wise to examine the annual publication of the state organization for more detailed discussion of the organization's activities and information about key officers and members.

County histories also provide crucial information about social activities of farm families. For example, the *History of Black Hawk County Iowa and Representative Citizens* (1911) included the following information about the local grange:

The grange movement reached this county in 1872–73, when the whole country seemed to be swept with the wave. The "Patrons of Husbandry," which was the name and designation given the grange movement, were nowhere better organized than in this county. Subordinate granges were started in every township and farmers and their wives crowded the regular meetings.

The underlying principle was that of cooperation, the elimination of the middlemen and the absorption into the coffers of the grange of the vast profits which the middlemen were supposed to enjoy. The reasoning was simple and plain; with these additions to their profits they would be able in a short time to pay off mortgages, improve their farms and become not only independent but a power able to protect their interest from all mercenary legislation which might be instigated by soulless corporations. There were cool-headed ones who, while they took part in the movement, had little faith in the grange as a miracle wonder worker capable of setting aside the natural laws of trade and producing a financial millennium, but the mass of the farming community, and many small traders in the towns who hoped in some way to reap benefit from it, were enthusiastic over the good they felt sure was in it for them.

The farmers' co-operative store was started in Waterloo on the East Side and on the West Side a co-operative elevator. Those were years of extreme depression and the embarrassed farmers grasped at anything which offered relief.

The order, according to some writers, was designed to secure social advantages and, if that were true, if it had adhered to the idea there is little doubt but it would have resulted in much good and may in some form have become a fixed social asset with the farming community. But if merely social advantages were its prime object, the prime object was so soon lost sight of in the ambition to make it the instrument of money making and a force in politics.

The business enterprises the grange engaged in were uniformly failures. It was impossible to satisfy, in management, such a mass of diversified tastes, business opinions and differing judgements as were embodied in the membership. The store and elevator had but a brief existence; the membership rapidly shrank after the first excitement had subsided and very little if anything remained of it in Black Hawk County 10 years after its institution there.

This passage from the county history provides several important leads. First, the Grange quickly became something more than the social and educational association that Kelley had planned. Cooperative buying and selling became the overriding purpose of the organization, but those efforts soon failed. The inquisitive historian will now pursue the kinds of business activities that were important to the grangers in the state as well as in the county and township of the farm. Important questions include the following: Who were the local leaders? Did the family who operated the farm join the organization? Women were admitted to the Grange. Did the woman of the house participate? How did her membership differ from her husband's participation? What did grangers discuss at their meetings? What were the results? Today, the Patrons of Husbandry remains an active farmers' organization. Current and past operators of the farm could be asked whether they belong to it. If so, one might inquire about their activities on the local level, the work of the national organization and its effects on them. If the present-day operator does not belong to the Grange, one might question why.

The Grange, of course, is just one example of the many agricultural organizations that may have been important to the families who have lived on the farm. Both written and oral sources may identify other organizations, such as the American Farm Bureau Federation, National Farmers' Union, and National Farmers Organization. In some regions agricultural organizations, such as the Farmers' Alliance, Farmers' Holiday Association, and the American Agriculture Movement, had political as well as social and economic agendas. Others, such as the People's or Populist party, were political organizations from the beginning. The farm historian would be wise to determine the social, economic, and political organizations that have been important to the owners and operators of the farm over time in order to understand the inter-relationships and complexity of its history.

Newspapers and county histories can also provide information about the formation and membership of mutual fire insurance companies as well as the organization of county agricultural societies. Agricultural societies emerged during the eighteenth century for the purpose of improving farming practices. Men and women attended the meetings to hear lectures from outside experts or from the members about matters such as the best crop rotation patterns, new varieties of wheat, or improved breeding for the dairy herd. Besides the information garnered, these meetings gave farm families an opportunity to leave the work and isolation of the farm behind for a day or so, if possible, and meet with friends and neighbors to talk about daily affairs as well as farm improvements.

County agricultural societies invariably organized an annual agricultural fair, where judges awarded ribbons and monetary premiums for the best entries in a variety of exhibits, such as vegetables, pickles, pies, preserves, fine arts, and needle work as well as for the best exhibits of dairy cows, beef cattle, swine, and poultry. Fair time was another chance for farm families to take a break from work, visit with friends, and increase their knowledge about the best agricultural practices. In relation to local fairs, agricultural societies, and organizations, the historian will do well to discover the kinds of organizational activities that farm owners or operators joined from the earliest date for which there is evidence to the present. These organizational activities will help the historian understand the daily concerns of the men, women, and children who lived on the farm.

CHURCHES AND SCHOOLS

If a country church stands nearby, the farm historian should try to determine whether the families who lived on the farm were members, whether they attended a church in town, or whether they avoided religion. The historian, of course, can ask the current occupants of the farm about church membership, but this may be too personal a question for a family that does not know the researcher. If the farm remains in the family of the historian, of course, church membership or affilia-

Agricultural photographs often can be dramatic. Here, a group of farmers stand before an auctioneer at a foreclosure sale during the 1930s in Iowa. Notice the National Guard troops and the machine gunner behind the auctioneer all of whom are poised to intimidate and keep order. Some of these farmers probably were members of the Farmers' Holiday Association, while most were sympathetic with its cause, especially the need to halt farm foreclosures by any means. *Courtesy of the State Historical Society of Iowa.*

tion can be addressed more conveniently, and oral history may prove enlightening.

The historian should try to discover not only where the farm family or families attended church, but also the activities the institution sponsored. The goal, of course, is not to learn about theology, but rather to find out about the social activities of the farm family over time. What were the special church meetings and celebrations that drew farm families together? What has been the significance of births, deaths, baptisms, marriages, and special holidays to the family not only privately but also in the broader social context of sharing with friends and relatives? What did these events mean to the family and life on the farm?

Some of these questions can be answered by oral history, but the researcher will need to consult the family Bible, which often served as a place to record important family events, as well as the records of the church. Sometimes the church records will be in the possession of that denomination's archives or in the local administrative office. In either case the researcher will need to ask for permission to use these records. James P. Wind, *Places of Worship: Exploring Their History* (Nashville: American Association of State and Local History, 1990) can provide guidance.

Similarly, a country school probably served the farm at some time. If the building no longer remains, the local historian should try to determine where it was located and how long it served the children raised on the farm. The researcher should also try to determine the curriculum and the names of the teachers who taught the farm's children. The impact of school consolidation may also be worth examining. For an excellent introduction to conducting research on local school history see Ronald E. Butchart, *Local Schools: Exploring Their History* (Nashville: American Association for State and Local History, 1986). Wayne E. Fuller provides an important introduction to country schools in *The Old Country School: The Story of Rural Education in the Middle West* (Chicago: University of Chicago Press, 1982) and *The Story of Rural Education in the Middle West: An Illustrated History* (Lawrence: University Press of Kansas, 1994).

MATERIAL POSSESSIONS

The material possessions of a farm family can tell a great deal about wealth, social status, and everyday life. Beyond the observation of a farm's contemporary material standing, the historian will have to use

Country schools played an important social as well as educational role in the farm community. These children pose for the photographer outside their one-room school in South Dakota near the turn of the twentieth century. Their formal clothing suggests a special occasion. *Photo courtesy of South Dakota State Historical Society—State Archives.*

probate records to answer questions about the economic wealth and accompanying social status of the farm family. First, the historian needs to identify the names of the owners or operators of the farm over time. Then, the researcher must determine the date of death of various owners. This information can be obtained from letters, diaries, newspapers, and oral history.

Probate records itemize the possessions of the owner of the farm and their value at the time of death. The researcher may wish to photocopy or record this information by hand to enable study later. The following list of household possessions comes from the 1858 probate records of John Locke Hardeman, whose farm equipment inventory was noted earlier:

1 Wardrobe	$ 20.00
1 Clock	10.00
1 Table with drawers	8.00
Washstand	2.00
Lounge	4.00
Small table with drawers	4.00

trunks	5.00
medicine chest & medicines	5.00
Library and map	200.00
1 washbowl foot tub	2.00
1 watch	75.00
2 guns	20.00
1 clock	90.00
Silver ware	92.00
German silver spoons	1.00
Knives & forks	13.00
13 candlesticks	3.25
Dishes plates & so forth	15.00
1 set china	25.00
1 Lot stone china	15.00
1 " Glassware	7.00
Lamp	1.00
Stove	12.00
Wash stand & Bowl	6.00
Bed Stead & Bedding	10.00
bed Linen in closet	13.00
Carpet	8.00
Parlor furniture	199.00
Hat rack	5.00
1 Set stone china	7.00
Bedstead bedding and trundle bed	10.00
1 wash stand and bowl	2.25
1 hall Lamp	3.00
1 Bureau	22.00
Wash stand bowl & rack	8.00
1 Stove	15.00
bedstead and bedding	13.00
bed clothing in closet	42.00
1 carpet	20.00
1 glass	.25
6 feather beds in the attic	75.00
26 pr shoes	45.00
2 doz windsor chairs	18.00
1/2 doz split bottom "	4.50
1/3 [doz.] dining "	19.00
2 Lots Skillets Iron pots etc.	16.75
Cooking utensils etc.	7.00

Probate records, then, enable the historian to evaluate the material possessions in an intimate way and draw conclusions about the wealth and social status of the farm operator and his or her family.

TRANSPORTATION AND COMMUNICATION

Although most farms were isolated at some time during their history, improved roads increased communication and trade with nearby marketing towns and villages and enhanced the social contacts of farm families. The farm historian will do well to pursue the changes in transportation and communication that affected farm life. Specifically, the historian should determine whether a canal or railroad served the neighborhood of the farm. If so, he or she can gain further insight by determining the circumstances of that construction and the benefits that the canal or railroad brought to the farm. Research on canals will necessarily be conducted in the written records, but oral history will help with the significance of a railroad to the farm.

Similarly, during the late nineteenth and early twentieth centuries, farmers demanded the free delivery of their mail as well as parcel post service, and Congress slowly responded. The farm historian should determine when the farm began receiving mail and package deliveries. These were important services, because they brought the outside world to the farm family's gate. Farmers no longer had to go to town to collect their mail at the post office. Yet, instead of increasing isolation rural free delivery and parcel post service improved contact with the world beyond the farm. Newspapers, for example, arrived more promptly and farm families could order needed equipment and household items from catalogs such as Sears, Roebuck and Montgomery Ward. At the same time, farm families began to demand the improvement of roads in order to ensure delivery of the mail and county, state, and federal governments responded by funding improvements which became part of the Good Roads movement during the early twentieth century. The historian could profit from learning how these services and changes affected the farm. Wayne E. Fuller provides an excellent history of rural free delivery in *RFD: The Changing Face of Rural America* (Bloomington: Indiana University Press, 1966), and "The Farmers' Mail: RFD," *Timeline* 4 (April–May 1987): 30–41.

Similarly, during the 1920s many farm families acquired their first radio. Quickly, radios became necessities rather than luxuries. With a radio farm families could get important marketing and weather information as well as news from across the nation and around the world.

Changes in transportation have affected farms over time. These children are riding in a "school wagon" near Popular Springs, Georgia, about 1912. In little more than a generation, school buses provided the same service for farm children. *Courtesy of the Southern Historical Collection, Library of the University of North Carolina, Chapel Hill.*

Radios brought agricultural programs designed to improve farming practices along with music and sports programming into the home. Often farm families visited neighbors in the evenings in order to listen to the radio. As a result, radios increased social activities and significantly helped end rural isolation. The farm historian might investigate when radios, telephones, and televisions were first acquired and evaluate the effects of each on the history of the farm.

The historian would also do well to determine when the farm operators first acquired an automobile and to assess its influence on the farm family. The researcher should ask questions such as these: How did the automobile change farm life? Did it contribute to the employment of the family members off the farm? Who drove the automo-

The radio and telephone became important technological additions to the farm home. Each helped reduce rural isolation and fundamentally changed the lives of country people. *Courtesy of the United States Department of Agriculture.*

bile—the senior man or woman of the house? For what purposes was the automobile used? How have those uses changed over time?

LABOR

Labor has always been essential to the success of any farm, but it is easy to overlook farm workers when writing the history of a farm, particularly if only family labor is involved. Yet, agricultural labor relationships are complex, and the historian must sort them out. Specifically, she or he needs to determine which tasks were divided by gender and age over the history of the farm. Did women, for example, milk, or was this a task reserved for the males of the household? Similarly, did the women drive the tractor at plowing time, haul wheat or corn to market in a wagon or truck, or tend poultry and the garden?

Children have always been important to the farm for their labor. In 1922, these children harvested sugar beets in western Kansas. *Kansas State Historical Society.*

What were the work responsibilities of the children? How did those responsibilities change over time?

In writing the history of a truck or large-scale corporate farm where extensive outside labor has been employed annually, the researcher is obliged to ask different questions. For example, did the farm employ migrant workers? If so, what was their nationality? Has that nationality changed over time? How were the workers employed—through a state or private employment service or privately by the owner? What provisions were made for their shelter? When were they paid? How much were they paid? Did the owner experience any labor problems such as strikes or other unrest among the workers? If so, how were those problems resolved? How has outside labor contributed to the successes or failures of the farm?

The farm historian should seek out both written and oral sources for the study of agricultural labor. Letters and diaries will be important as well as local newspaper accounts of labor shortages, employment practices, and problems. Oral histories may also prove valuable. The historian will achieve the fullest picture by interviewing both employers and workers.

ENTERTAINMENT

Although farm families have often been relatively isolated, at least until they bought an automobile, they still managed to enjoy a wide range of entertainment activities. In addition to socialization at Grange meetings and the county fairs, farm women often got together regularly to make quilts and enjoy each other's company. Farm women sometimes also participated in organizations called Ladies' Aid Societies. Members met at a home, held a brief religious service, took up a collection to support an important cause, ate refreshments, and visited a few hours while they worked on their sewing.

Church and school socials and activities also provided entertainment throughout the year. Moreover, during the nineteenth and early twentieth centuries, the Chautauqua provided entertainment for farm and town families. The Chautauqua was a service that scheduled speakers such as Clarence Darrow, musical groups such as the Swiss Bell Ringers, and theatrical performers for appearances across rural America. The farm historian may wish to try to determine the types of Chautauqua performances that visited the locality of the farm and look for evidence that the farm family attended.

Sunday dinner was also a time of socialization and a form of entertainment for farm families. Often friends and relatives were invited for Sunday dinner, which was served at mid-day or early afternoon. On those occasions, the farm wife and her daughters prepared a large meal from home-produced foods. This meal differed little from daily meals except that more food was prepared and a few delicacies set out. After dinner, the men customarily moved to the parlor or to the barnyard to look over the livestock while the women washed the dishes. In either case, Sunday dinner proved an important social occasion for the hosts and the guests. Both written records and oral history may help with this research.

The farm historian can profitably investigate other kinds of entertainment activities that the farm families enjoyed. This research might include asking whether they attend weekly sales at the local auction barn or nearby farm auctions. For the nineteenth and early twentieth centuries, the farm historian may be able to find written records that shed light on the entertainment and social experience of the corn harvest, threshing time, barn raising, or butchering day, when friends and neighbors commonly contributed their time and labor to help a farm family complete an important task in a necessarily brief amount of time. Oral history also might be helpful.

Before many women took off-the-farm employment after 1950, they often organized social clubs. Meeting once a month, they engaged in social interaction by playing cards, eating lunch, or working on a special project. These organizations played an important role in reducing rural isolation. *Courtesy of the United States Department of Agriculture.*

WRITTEN REFLECTIONS

The task of the farm historian, then, is to draw on a variety of research techniques to write the history of a farm. The daily life of the farm, over time, is important to that story. The historian might also ask the family members who currently live on the farm as well as those who have done so in the past, to talk or write about a specific farm activity, such as raising poultry, harvesting corn, supervising hired workers, cooking for threshing crews, participating in organized activities, such as the Grange, or attending a country school.

Written reflections about farm life can be significant to the historian. In this example, a farmer in southern Ohio writes about the activities required to produce a tobacco crop in 1983. His reflection is

Farm families have often joined agricultural organizations to improve their knowledge and increase their social activities. On August 14, 1949, these members of the Iowa Southern Aberdeen Angus Association gathered on a farm near Osceola for a picnic. *Photo Courtesy State Historical Society of Iowa—Des Moines.*

helpful. Note the important references to weather, technology, labor, prices, and tradition, all of which will be of consequence for the historian who writes the history of the farm.

Various generations of my family have been tobacco growers. . . . My ancestors came to America from Ireland and Scotland in the seventeenth century and prospered in tobacco production, early on in North Carolina, and later in Kentucky. Today, my family grows tobacco in southern Ohio, where tobacco production is nearly as important as corn or bean production.

Among Ohio tobacco producers, burley and broadleaf types are the most popular and profitable to produce, and are also best-suited for Ohio's weather and soil conditions.

Also, tobacco growing is regulated by the federal government. The Department of Agriculture sets poundage limits on the production of these farmers authorized to grow tobacco. This poundage limit is known as the tobacco *base*, a limit which cannot be exceeded by more than fifteen percent. Each year, a new base is set, based on the past year's production. If a farmer chooses not to grow tobacco, he could lose his base altogether, and thus lose his authorization to produce tobacco.

As with any crop, a lot of time goes into preparing for the tobacco planting season. Early in the year, the federal government sends out tobacco base limits. Farmers generally set aside about one acre for every 2,000 pounds of tobacco base. With this information, farmers choose good land where adequate sunlight and drainage exist, and prepare the fields through plowing, disking, and proper fertilization.

Once plantbeds are prepared, a broadcast spreader is used to plant a mixture of tiny tobacco seeds and fertilizer (tobacco seeds resemble finely ground pepper). Once planting is complete, the plantbeds are covered for several weeks by large sheets of cheesecloth or other similar material to protect the plants (actually seedlings at this point) from heavy rains, late frost, and strong, direct sunlight.

When the tobacco plants are about six inches tall, they are pulled from the plantbeds and transplanted into the well-fertilized larger fields. Pulling plants for transplant is done by hand, but the actual transplanting is made easier by a tractor-pulled contraption called a tobacco setter.

Usually, many plants must be set by hand, also. This occurs mostly at the end of rows where tractors have limited space and must leave room to turn around, but occasionally a plant will have to be added in the middle of a row where the two people riding the setter missed a pincher on the wheel and nothing was planted. Planting by hand simply involves poking a hole in the ground, inserting a plant, and adding a little water. This is fine for small jobs, but the setter saves much time and strain. I can't believe that my ancestors set by hand well into the 1950s.

Once the plants get large enough so that tractors can no longer get into the fields without damaging them, the only way to safely get rid of weeds is by hoeing or by pulling them out by hand. This is not a big job if one doesn't wait until a major weed problem arises to start hoeing.

Weather can be just as tough on plants as are diseases and insects. Hail and heavy rains can not only knock plants down, but the rains can also drown a crop if adequate drainage isn't available. Lack of adequate sunlight can lead to shorter, lighter plants. On the other hand, too much sunlight after a lot of rain can lead to scalding, a problem where the plants wilt and turn yellow, not unlike a sunburn.

Before cutting begins, tobacco sticks must be dropped end-to-end down the length of every other row. Tobacco sticks are wooden sticks about a yard in length and about as thick as a broomstick.

Each person cutting the tobacco is armed with a light-weight hatchet, which is used to cut the stalk at the base of the plant. Taking two rows at a time, each cutter works a row full of tobacco sticks.

With a row on each side to cut, a tobacco cutter must first jab the closest tobacco stick into the ground so it stands upright. He then puts a small, cone-shaped spear on the upraised end of the stick. Then, he begins cutting the stalks and spearing them into the sticks. Each stick will have from five to eight stalks, depending on the size of the plants. Most experienced cutters do uniform work; they cut and spear three plants from their left side then three plants from their right side, then move on to the next stick, put it into the ground, add the spear on the top end, and commence to cutting.

This cutting usually, weather permitting, goes on until the entire field is cut. Then, the freshly cut tobacco is left in the field (on the sticks) to wilt and cure for a few hours.

The sticks of tobacco (remember now, the stalks are speared onto the sticks) are then loaded onto a wagon or truck and taken to a well-ventilated barn or shed where the sticks are hung on tier poles and rails to dry and cure. Hanging is done from the top of the barn to the bottom tier, which should not touch the ground, until the barn is full, or until there is no more tobacco to hang. Each stick is hung between two rails (a barn may have many, many rails), and each stick is spaced from four to twelve inches (six inches apart is average) apart to allow good circulation of air around each plant on each stick. As each stick is hung, the plants on the stick are evenly spread so as to further promote even drying and curing. Air should be allowed to flow freely through tobacco barns, but the tobacco should never be put in a place where rain or other precipitation can reach it.

Tobacco is left to dry in the barns for anywhere from six to twelve weeks. In this time, the tobacco turns from a dark green at cutting time, to yellow, then to a rich, dark brown, and the leaves go from tough and pliable to comparatively fragile.

Once the tobacco is cured uniformly, it is then prepared for market. This effort begins by bringing the sticks of tobacco out of the barn and into a small, heated room called a stripping shed. The tobacco is then taken off the stick and thrown into one pile, while the sticks are thrown into another pile (empty, of course).

Then, the people working in the stripping shed do what the word suggests, they strip the tobacco off of the stalks. They either strip the leaves by grade, that is, they strip the large bottom leaves, then the middle leaves, then the small top leaves, or they strip the leaves all in one grade, as is most common today.

Most tobacco farmers used to take the stripped leaves and tie them into small hand-sized bundles, then drape the hand bundles over loose tobacco sticks and put the stick into small wall presses. From the small presses, the stripped tobacco (now on a stick, again) was put into large bulk presses, where they would remain until the tobacco was sold.

Today, most tobacco farmers in Ohio simply strip one grade of tobacco and put it into small box-shaped presses lined with two strands of rope or twine. When the box is full and the contents pressed as full as it can go, the strings are tied, and the side of the box press is removed. You are now ready to pull out a 50 to 100 pound, ready for market bale of burley.

Tobacco is sold at large tobacco warehouses which are open for farmers and their product from about Thanksgiving to about the middle of February. Most farmers move their tobacco to market in pickup trucks, although some use large-bed trailers or wagons.

Prices given for tobacco vary by type and demand. Generally, burley sells for $1.50 to $2.00 per pound (remember, decent tobacco runs about 2,000 pounds per acre), and broadleaf sells for $.40 to $1.25 per pound. This is why burley is more popular among farmers than broadleaf, despite lesser government regulation for broadleaf (the base for burley is allotted; broadleaf can be grown in any quantity as long as you sign up for a certain number of pounds and do not exceed by more than 10–15 percent the amount signed up for). Thus, for the same work, burley is far more profitable. Most farmers grow broadleaf simply for extra income.

After the tobacco is taken to market (sometimes in one trip, and sometimes in many trips over many weeks), preparation is made for the new crop season. Barns are prepared, fields are plowed, and repairs or replacements are made on tools and machinery. Even the stripped tobacco stalks have a purpose. They are spread onto the fields, where, plowed under, they make a good form of fertilizer. Not always, but generally, nothing goes to waste on the farm, and that goes double for time, especially when there is work to do, which there almost always is.

In comparatively poor ground (compared to, say, central Ohio, for example), southern Ohio farmers find tobacco to be far more profitable per acre than soybeans. For example, one acre of good beans will bring about 40 bushels at $6.00 per bushel. For sewing and harvesting the acre, you make $240 before expenses. One good acre of burley, on the other hand, will bring in 2,000 pounds at about $1.80 (remember, these are just examples, but, I believe, fair and typical ones). For your hard work and persistence, you make $3,600 on your acre before expenses, of which labor is usually the largest. Any way you look at it, it is obvious that money can be *earned* by growing tobacco. Even 500 pounds of broadleaf at $.50 earns $250, and to get it you would only use about a third of an acre for tobacco.

There can be no question that tobacco growing requires a lot of man-hours and hard work. The big payoff looms as good incentive.

Perhaps the most overlooked reason why farmers, especially southern Ohio farmers, grow tobacco is an intangible—tradition. For many, tobacco growing is a way of life—just too good to give up.

Willing individuals can provide excellent written reflections about a host of daily farm activities. The key is to ask them to address precise and limited questions or to write about specific events or activities. Then, the historian can take notes from these documents and refer to both when writing the history of the farm.

LIVING HISTORICAL FARMS

The historian will find living historical farms to be important places to gain a better understanding of agricultural practices con-

ducted during certain ages of the past. Living historical farms are ex-
tensions of open air museums such as Colonial Williamsburg in Virginia and Old Sturbridge Village in Massachusetts. Living historical
farms are a unique type of agricultural museum because they do what
indoor museums cannot and what most open air museums do not do:
they show what has always been most important about agriculture—
the actual tending of living plants and animals. Living historical
farms exhibit the husbandry of some specific time in the past by dem-
onstrating the tools and implements, livestock and poultry breeds,
and plant varieties characteristic of a specific time period. Some living
historical farms such as Mount Vernon, George Washington's home in
Virginia, and Lincoln's boyhood home in Indiana, portray life during
the time and place of residence of a notable person. Others, such as
Colonial Pennsylvania, the Iowa Living History Farms, and Old
Cienega Village near Santa Fe, New Mexico, depict agricultural practices in a general location and period.

The emphasis at living historical farms is on the farming process
itself. These museums help correct misconceptions about agriculture
that have developed over time, particularly because farming has been
romanticized as more and more people have left it for urban America.
Living historical farms simply re-create the past as accurately as possible and acknowledge the problems that farm men, women, and children faced while living on the land during a certain time. In addition,
however, living historical farms also have been the first agricultural
museums to collect animals and plants with the intent of exhibiting
them along with tools and implements in a functional setting. By so
doing, living historical farms uniquely portray farm life, which even
in its most recent form is beyond the personal experience of most
Americans. Moreover, besides functioning as public educational cen-
ters, some living historical farms such as the National Colonial Farm
in Maryland and the Freeman Farm at Old Sturbridge Village have be-
gun developing plant varieties and breeding animals representative of
a specific time in the past.

Living historical farms enable visitors to reflect on their rural past.
By viewing objects, demonstrations, and farm settings, visitors can
more fully understand their ethnological background, their nation's
social and technological development, and the agricultural practices
of their ancestors. As a result, they can better comprehend the process
of agricultural development and the nature of farm life. Agricultural
museums also offer farm historians an exciting opportunity for social,
economic, cultural, technological, and environmental research. At living historical farms the historian can learn why and how farm fami-

lies conducted certain activities in the past. A visit to a living historical farm will help the historian put her or his own research in perspective and contribute to the crafting of a vibrant farm history.

Anyone wanting to visit a living historical farm will find the following directories helpful: *Selected Living Historical Farms, Villages and Agricultural Museums in the United States and Canada* (Washington, DC: Association for Living Historical Farms and Agricultural Museums, n.d.); *Farm Museum Directory: A Guide Through America's Farm Past* (Lancaster, PA: Stemgas Pub. Co., 1986); and Sam Rosenberg, *Travel Historic Rural America: A Guide to Agricultural Museums and Events in the U.S. and Canada* (St. Joseph, MI: American Society of Agricultural Engineers, 1982).

৵৹

FOODWAYS

The historian may find the study of foodways on the farm a profitable area for investigation. The preservation and preparation of food can tell the historian much about ethnicity, economic status, technology, diet, and nutrition on the farm over time as well as about food production. Recipes and references to canning and other food preservation techniques in family letters and diaries in addition to oral histories can be helpful for research.

In the study of the farm's foodways the historian should also ask a variety of questions. For example: What have been the most common dishes prepared on the farm? How have those dishes changed through the years? Did changes in the farm's agricultural emphasis alter the foodways of the families who have lived there? How have changes in transportation, technology, and food preservation influenced the foodways of the farm? What foods have commonly been purchased? Has ethnicity influenced the farm's foodways? Does ethnicity remain important for food preparation on the farm? What can be said about diet and nutrition for the families who have lived on the farm?

The following two studies by Harvey A. Levenstein are useful places to begin for the historian who is interested in conducting research on the foodways of the farm: *Paradox of Plenty: A Social History of Eating in Modern America* (New York: Oxford University Press, 1993) and *Revolution at the Table: The Transformation of American Diet* (New York: Oxford University Press, 1988). See also Sarah F. McMahon, "A Comfortable Subsistence: The Changing Composition of Diet in Rural New England, 1620–1840," *William and Mary Quarterly*, 3d ser., 42 (January 1985): 26–65, and Sam B.

Hilliard, "Hog Meat and Cornpone: Foodways in the Antebellum South," in *Material Life in America, 1600–1860,* edited by Robert Blair St. George, 311–32 (Boston: Northeastern University Press, 1988).

RANCHING

Ranches are important subjects for research by historians who are exploring nearby history. Ranches differ from farms with their emphasis on livestock production, usually cattle. Ranches often, but not always, have more acres than farms to permit widespread grazing as well as the raising of hay, grain, and forage crops. The research techniques that the historian uses to investigate the past of a farm can also be used to pursue the history of a ranch. Moreover, both farms and ranches should be considered part of the general development of American agriculture.

The ranch historian, however, will also need to ask other questions. Important areas for study will include the manner of land acquisition. If the ranch is located in California or the Southwest, it probably was a part of a Spanish or Mexican land grant. Many ranches in the Far West have cultural origins in Spain regarding the techniques and vocabulary of ranching. Yet some ranchers on the Great Plains use British techniques and vocabulary. The ranch historian, then, will do well to investigate the cultural heritage of the ranch.

The ranch historian might also study the manner in which breeding, grazing, feeding, branding, marketing, and labor techniques of the ranch have changed over time. Have the owners of the ranch, for example, changed breeds to accommodate the climate and consumer demands? Does the ranch purchase calves for fattening from Mexican cattle raisers or other ranchers or farmers? Where is the market for the cattle? How have government programs affected livestock raising on the ranch? Does the ranch produce supplemental feed for fattening the cattle? Or, does the ranch emphasize grass fattening until the cattle are ready for finishing on corn in feedlots in other areas? What have been the environmental effects of the ranch, if feedlots are part of the operation? How has the technology of the ranch changed over time?

Ranch historians will profit from begining their research by reading Terry G. Jordan, *North American Cattle-Ranching Frontiers: Origins, Diffusion, and Differentiation* (Albuquerque: University of New Mexico

Press, 1993). This study is the most recent and authoritative book about the history of ranching in the United States. Two other useful studies are: Sandra L. Myers, *The Ranch in Spanish Texas, 1691–1800* (El Paso: Texas Western Press, 1969) and Walter Prescott Webb, *The Great Plains* (1931; reprint, Lincoln: University of Nebraska Press, 1981).

FARM FICTION

Historians will find fiction useful in their research to help them understand the everyday details of farm life as well as the attitudes, beliefs, and habits of rural people in a particular time and place. Attributes of farm people, such as conservatism, individualism, anti-intellectualism, and hostility to government, industry, and cities as well as generosity, neighborliness, and perseverance, often can be identified and evaluated within the context of fiction. Fiction, of course, cannot be used to obtain facts about a particular farm, but the historian can use it to understand regional characteristics, social trends, and cultural changes relating to agriculture in a general area. Fiction can also help the historian understand the relationship of the environment to farm life and the personal identity of those who have lived on the land.

Erskine Caldwell's *Tobacco Road*, for example, presents a classic example of poverty-stricken sharecroppers in the South during the early twentieth century as well as the inability of some farmers to adjust to changing economic conditions. Equally, Frederick Manfred's *The Golden Bowl* provides insight to a farm family's trust and faith in the land during the Dust Bowl years of the 1930s. Hamlin Garland's *Main-Travelled Roads* furnishes a glimpse of the privations and hardships faced by the men and women who settled on midwestern farms during the late nineteenth century, while Frank Norris's *The Octopus*, tells a story about the confrontational relationship between wheat growers and the railroad trust in California's San Joaquin Valley at the turn of the twentieth century. John Steinbeck, of course, gives an unparalleled description of the migration to California by cotton tenant farmers who lost their leases in Oklahoma during the Great Depression in *The Grapes of Wrath*. Jane Smiley offers a critique of midwestern farm life that is often stereotyped as the epitome of stable, family-oriented, independent living. In her novel *A Thousand Acres*, Smiley portrays life on a farm during the late twentieth century, where hard work and family values are little more than myth, where the patriarch abuses the land and people, and where bankers and lawyers foster corruption—all of which contribute to the disintegration of the farm family.

Other important works of nonhistory that will help the researcher understand matters of time and place, immigration, settlement, and the relationship of farm families to nature and each other include Willa Cather's *O Pioneers!* and *My Antonia*, Mari Sandoz's, *Old Jules*, and O. E. Rölvaag's *Giants of the Earth*.

Farm historians who are interested in using fiction as a research tool should consult Janet M. Labrie, "The Depiction of Women's Field Work in Rural Fiction," *Agricultural History* 67 (Spring 1993): 119–33; Carole S. Manning, "Agrarianism, Female-Style," *Southern Quarterly* 30 (Winter–Spring 1992): 69–76; Carolyn Hlus, "The Changing Fictional Images of Women on the North American Landscape," *Canadian Review of American Studies* 17 (Fall 1986): 347–54. See also Roy W. Meyer, *The Middle Western Farm Novel in the Twentieth Century* (Lincoln: University of Nebraska Press, 1965) and Caroline B. Sherman, "The Development of American Rural Fiction," *Agricultural History* 12 (January 1938): 67–76.

The research needs of the farm historian, then, will be determined by the particular farm under study and the people who lived on it. Daily life on farms is complex, and to understand its significance to the history of the farm the historian is best advised to use a number of research techniques and ask a host of questions about a variety of topics. The work can be time consuming and even difficult, but the rewards will be immeasurable.

SUGGESTED READINGS

The best introductions to everyday life, including farm life, are John W. Dodds, *Everyday Life in Twentieth Century America* (New York: G. P. Putnam's Sons, 1965); Harvey Green, *The Uncertainty of Everyday Life, 1915–1945* (New York: HarperCollins, 1992); David Freeman Hawke, *Everyday Life in Early America* (New York: Harper and Row, 1988); Jack Larkin, *The Reshaping of Everyday Life, 1790–1840* (New York: Harper and Row, 1988); John C. Miller, *The First Frontier: Life in Colonial America* (New York: Dell, 1966); Malcolm J. Rohrbough, *The Trans-Appalachian Frontier: People, Societies, and Institutions, 1775–1850* (New York: Oxford University Press, 1978); Thomas J. Schlereth, *Victorian America: Transformation in Everyday Life, 1876–1915* (New York: HarperCollins, 1991); Daniel E. Sutherland, *The Expansion of Everyday Life, 1860–1876* (New York: Harper and Row, 1989); and Louis B. Wright, *Everyday Life in Colonial America* (New York: G. P. Putnam's

Sons, 1965). See also Stephanie Grauman Wolf, *As Various as Their Land: The Everyday Lives of Eighteenth-Century Americans* (New York: HarperCollins, 1993). An excellent introduction to migration and inheritance as factors that influence farm life is Hal S. Barron, *Those Who Stayed Behind: Rural Society in Nineteenth-Century New England* (Cambridge: Cambridge University Press, 1984).

More specialized studies of everyday farm life include Nicholas P. Hardeman, *Shucks, Shocks, and Hominy Blocks: Corn as a Way of Life in Pioneer America* (Urbana: University of Illinois Press, 1975) and David E. Schob, *Hired Hands and Plow Boys: Farm Labor in the Midwest, 1815–1950* (Urbana: University of Illinois Press, 1975). Mark Friedberger discuss major changes in California and Iowa that will suggest areas for research in other regions in *Farm Families and Change in the Twentieth Century* (Lexington: University Press of Kentucky, 1988). For an excellent study of daily concerns, such as veterinary practices, fencing problems, swindlers, and patent controversies see Earl W. Hayter, *The Troubled Farmer, 1850–1900* (DeKalb: Northern Illinois University Press, 1973). See also Leslie Mina Prosterman, *Ordinary Life: Aesthetics in the Midwestern County Fair* (Washington, DC: Smithsonian Institution Press, 1995).

The daily activities of farm women are discussed in Joan Jensen, *Loosening the Bonds: Mid-Atlantic Farm Women, 1750–1850* (New Haven: Yale University Press, 1986); Elizabeth Fox-Genovese, *Within the Plantation Household: Black and White Women in the Old South* (Chapel Hill: University of North Carolina Press, 1988); "Women in Agriculture during the Nineteenth Century," in *Agriculture and National Development: Views of the Nineteenth Century*, ed. Lou Ferleger, 267–301 (Ames: Iowa State University Press, 1990); and Rachel Ann Rosenfeld, *Farm Women: Work, Farm, and Family in the United States* (Chapel Hill: University of North Carolina Press, 1985). An excellent diary by a farm woman in Ohio that also will suggest further research is *Farm Wife: A Self-Portrait, 1886–1896*, ed. Virginia E. McCormick (Ames: Iowa State University Press, 1990). For a similar diary for a farmer on the Great Plains see Janet M. Neugebaur, *Plains Farmer: The Diary of William G. DeLoach, 1914–1964* (College Station: Texas A & M University Press, 1991). A useful diary with an Iowa location is H. Roger Grant, ed., *Years of Struggle: The Farm Diary of Elmer A. Powers, 1931–1936* (Ames: Iowa State University Press, 1976). Floyd A. Robinson provides a reconstruction or portrayal of a typical midwestern farm during the second and third decades of the twentieth century in *This Is Home Now* (Ames: Iowa State University Press, 1983).

The everyday relations of farm families with nearby merchants and communities is treated succinctly by Lewis Atherton in *The Frontier Merchant in Mid-America* (Columbia: University of Missouri Press, 1971), *The Southern Country Store, 1800–1860* (Baton Rouge: Louisiana University Press, 1949) and *Main Street on the Middle Border* (Bloomington: Indiana University Press, 1954).

For the social consequences of technological change see Don F. Hadwiger and Clay Cochran, "Rural Telephones in the United States," *Agricultural History* 58 (July 1984): 221–38, and two articles by Reynold M. Wik, "The Radio in Rural America During the 1920s," *Agricultural History* 55 (October 1981): 339–50 and "The USDA and the Development of Radio in Rural America," *Agricultural History* 62 (Spring 1988): 177–88.

The social importance of harvest time is shown in Thomas D. Isern, *Custom Combining on the Great Plains: A History* (Norman: University of Oklahoma Press, 1981) and J. Sanford Rikoon, *Threshing in the Midwest, 1820–1940* (Bloomington: Indiana University Press, 1988).

A useful, brief introduction to farmers' organizations, both political and labor, is Patrick H. Mooney and Theo J. Majka, *Farmers' and Farm Workers' Movements: Social Protest in American Agriculture* (New York: Twayne, 1995). See also Dick Meister and Anne Loftis, *A Long Time Coming: The Struggle to Unionize America's Farm Workers* (New York: Macmillan, 1977).

Chapter 6

THE FARMSTEAD

The history of buildings and gardens is an important aspect of any farm study. Indeed, the architectural evolution of the farmstead can reveal a great deal about agricultural change over time. The buildings on the farm at any particular time served specific purposes and more often than not were located in a particular site for a reason. Simply put, form followed function as farmers built their barns based on whether they raised a variety of crops and livestock or specialized in the production of certain crops and livestock. The function, size, and number of buildings varied from farm to farm and from one agricultural region to the next. The architecture of barns and other farmstead buildings also depended on topography and the ethnicity of the farmers and builders. Moreover, each generation made its mark on the farmstead. Change occurred naturally over time. Consequently, the architecture of the farmstead reflects the major activities and concerns of the families who have lived on the farm. Indeed, the house, barn, and outbuildings provided the focal point of daily farm life.

Barn styles tell much about climate, weather, crop and livestock production, and ethnic settlement patterns. The farmsteads of dairy and tobacco farmers necessarily were different. Similarly, while the nineteenth-century Virginia rail fence became popular in the South, and barbed wire fences throughout the West, the stone fence remained a traditional sight in New England. In Ohio, farmers crafted cabins from logs; in Nebraska they built houses from sod. In all cases, then, the architecture of the farmstead can help the historian understand the environmental, cultural, and economic determinants that caused those who lived on the farm to build and arrange structures in certain ways. Consequently, to know the farmstead is to know the people who lived there and their agricultural history.

Letters, diaries, and published reminiscences can help identify the sources of farm architecture. In 1895, for example, William Cooper

107

Howells reflected about his life in Jefferson County, Ohio, in *Recollections of Life in Ohio,* from 1813 to 1840 (Cincinnati, 1895), and he described the three-bay, double-pen barn that his family built soon after the War of 1812. Howells wrote:

> This summer we also built a barn of logs. . . . There were two pens put up twenty-four feet apart, and raised on one foundation. . . . They were in this way carried up to a proper height, when they were connected by logs and a common roof. This made a double barn, with stabling and more room at each end, and a barn floor and wagon-shed in the middle. Such was the universal style of barns in that country. . . .
>
> The settlers were mainly from western Pennsylvania, though many had come in from the western part of Maryland and Virginia, and the prevailing nationality was the Scotch-Irish of the second generation. . . .

Reminiscences such as Howells's can be invaluable to the historian studying farm architecture. The physical structure of the barn can also tell much about the builders, available construction materials, the amount of land cultivated, and the number and kind of livestock raised.

Architectural historians have not agreed on a single, comprehensive guideline for the classification of barns. Even so, the following description and illustrations of various forms of farmstead architecture will help the farm historian begin the task of building research. The suggested readings and the bibliographies and notes in these studies will take the researcher to the next, more advanced level of study.

BARNS

The barn usually dominates the farmstead. Generally during the frontier period, the barn was the first permanent structure built on the farm after the farmer had provided temporary shelter for himself and his family. The historian should ask: Where have the barns been located during the history of the farm? Manuscripts, diaries, letters, photographs, maps, and old foundations may show precise locations at both specific and general periods of time. Common sense will help as well because the barn had to be convenient to the farmhouse, but sufficiently far away to keep the flies, odor, and noise from interfering with family life as much as possible. Depending on the lay of the land and the purpose that it was to serve, a barn could be built either on a level area or on a hillside. The size of the barn indicates the farm's size and productive capacity. Large bank barns, for example, averaged between 80 and 100 feet in length, 40 to 60 feet wide, and about 50 feet high.

The architecture of barns often can tell the farm historian a great deal about ethnicity and settlement patterns in a rural neighborhood. In New England and the northern United States, including the Midwest, for example, European immigrants introduced the English, Dutch, and German barns. The English barn emerged from the British settlements in southern New England and the Chesapeake region, while the hearth for the German barn was the Delaware valley, and the Hudson River valley of New York and the Raritan River valley of New Jersey providing the area of origin for the Dutch barn. The barn types built in New England and the Midwest prior to World War II usually were variations of these three architectural styles. If not, the barns have been designed for specific agricultural purposes, such as curing tobacco.

The English barn, also known as the Yankee, Connecticut, or New England barn, had three bays or sections with the center large enough to accommodate a wagon. It consisted of a timber frame, gable roof, and double doors on the sides, not on the gable ends. Usually, these barns were one-and-a-half story structures with vertical pine board siding. Small gaps remained between the board siding to enable adequate ventilation, which helped prevent spontaneous combustion from the heat generated by the stored hay. Farmers threshed in the central bay, stored their sheaves and grain in the other bays, and pitched the straw into the hayloft.

The German or bank barns, which date to the late seventeenth century, are those that have been built against the side of a hill or which have a ramp that enables a team and wagon to reach the middle level. These barns have two-and-a-half stories. The farmer employed the lower level to shelter livestock, store grain, milk cows, and separate cream. He used the middle level to thresh and store grain and the upper level for a hayloft. This barn style is common in the eastern United States, particularly where dairying is important. The bank barn probably is a combination of German, Swiss, and Austrian architectural designs, and it evolved among immigrants in Pennsylvania and diffused into portions of the northern and midwestern United States.

The Sweitzer or Swisser barn is a variation of the German barn, and it is commonly seen from Pennsylvania to the Great Plains and from Virginia to Canada. This barn is a two-and-a-half story structure, but it has a distinctive forebay or overhang of six or more feet on the second level, where farmers often stored their grain in bins. A stone or brick wall usually supported the forebay. This overhang also provided

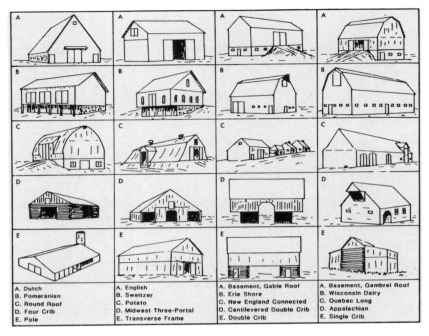

These barn styles have been popular among farmers in the northern United States. *Geographical Review (April 1982). Courtesy, American Geographical Society.*

protection for livestock below and enabled convenient feeding of cattle through doors cut in the floor. Many variations of this barn style remain throughout the Midwest, Pennsylvania, and Maryland.

The Dutch barns of the Northeast provide a strong cultural link to northern Europe, particularly the Netherlands, and indicate settlement patterns from the Hudson, Mohawk, and Schoharie river valleys to Long Island and northern New Jersey. These barns are large structures, whose builders used the same architectural principles of those who constructed the great cathedrals and basilicas of Europe. The Dutch barn can be distinguished from other styles by its distinctive sharp-pitched, gable roof, low eaves, and square floor plan. The roof is supported by interior posts rather than by the walls. Double doors occupy the center and single doors the corners at the gable ends. In contrast to the English and German barns, the siding on the Dutch structures was nailed horizontally to the frame rather than vertically, probably because farmers in seventeenth-century Holland joined their houses and barns and attached the horizontal siding. In America the

The English barn is a rectangular structure with a central floor and two side bays. These barns are also called double-crib and three-bay barns. Farmers threshed in the central bay and used the side bays to store grain and fodder and shelter livestock. *Courtesy of the Ohio Historical Society.*

Dutch separated their barns and houses but kept the horizontal siding tradition. The Dutch barn primarily served as a place to thresh wheat and other small grains as well as a storage facility for grain and hay. These barns were not well suited for sheltering livestock, and English barns began to surpass this architectural style during the late nineteenth and early twentieth centuries as farmers in this region began to emphasize dairying. Few original Dutch barns remain today, but barns patterned after this style can be found as far west as Michigan.

The English, German, and Dutch barns, then, were designed for specific purposes, and the historian should use these examples to help formulate and ask questions about the style, purpose, dating, and modification of barns on the farm under study. Farmers primarily used the English barn, for example, to thresh and store grain rather than to shelter livestock, such as dairy cows, swine, or horses. Modifications of this barn style often enable the sheltering of livestock in one of the three bays, but the style remains English in origin. Consequently, if an English barn is identified, the researcher can assume that the farmer who built it primarily emphasized small grain crops, such

The Sweitzer forebay barn frequently is called the German, Swiss, or Pennsylvania barn. Bank barns enabled farmers to shelter livestock on the lower level, gave easy access to the threshing floor on the center level, and provided a hayloft above. The German barn was one of the first used to store grain and shelter livestock. *Courtesy of the Ohio Historical Society.*

as wheat, barley, and oats or vegetable crops rather than cattle and hogs. Studies by geographers also indicate that the presence of English barns in New England and the Midwest suggest small-scale agricultural operations.

In contrast, farmers in Pennsylvania, Maryland, and New Jersey as well as Virginia and Wisconsin, adopted the German barn. This diffusion was the result of both German migration and the needs of farmers. As a result, few German barn styles exist where the German population remained small, such as along the Atlantic coast, in the Appalachian mountains, or near the Great Lakes. Moreover, dairy farmers needed a barn, such as the German style, to shelter their cows and provide room for storing hay and making butter and cheese.

Ohio provides an excellent example of German immigration and the spread of the traditional German barn style. German settlers made their way to western Ohio from approximately 1850 to 1890 and built large, frame barns with low-pitched roofs to house their livestock.

These barns often resemble the housebarns located along the North Sea in the German provinces. In Europe, the family lived in one end of the barn while the livestock occupied the other end. In Ohio, however, the settlers had more room because the acquisition of land proved easier and cheaper, and they did not need to live in the same dwelling with their cows and horses. As a result, they replicated their traditional barns, but they did not live in them. Thus, the style remained but the purpose or use of the German barn changed.

The farm historian may also come across other general barn designs. Crib barns, for example, while not as handsome as the English, German, or Dutch barns, are the simplest, and perhaps the oldest barn style in America. Crib barns have from one to four cribs or sections, which are also known as pens. A single door is located at a gable end. Farmers used crib barns to store ears of corn and to shelter a horse or cow. A small loft provided additional, though limited, storage space. On crib barns, the roof invariably is more substantial than the sides because it is more important to shelter livestock, grain, or implements from the rain than to keep out the cold. These barns primarily are found in the Appalachian region and throughout the Upper and Lower South and in the Chesapeake Bay area, although crib barns can also be found in other parts of the northern United States, such as Illinois, Michigan, and New York.

The Appalachian barn is a larger version of the crib barn. Farmers in Appalachia apparently developed this barn style, and it diffused from Virginia into Kentucky, Indiana, and Illinois. This barn style has an opening sufficiently large to enable the passage of a team of horses and a wagon along an interior aisle that runs from side to side near the front. This barn has a distinctive hayhood above the opening to the hayloft on the front. Typically, the Appalachian barn does not have a door on the end but rather on the side. These barns usually indicate small-scale and even subsistence agricultural operations.

Round barns originated about 1824. These barns were designed on the premise that round structures provided the farmer with more floor and less wall space than rectangular styles. Moreover, with the silo occupying the center of the barn, the feeding of livestock theoretically became easier and more efficient. During the 1880s octagonal barns became popular with many farmers who wanted to adopt a new barn style that supposedly offered greater efficiency in daily storage and feeding activities than round barns, but the round barn style returned to prominence during the first two decades of the twentieth century in the Midwest. By the 1930s, however, this architectural style had given way to more conventional crib barns because round barns did

John Johnston built this barn near Piqua, Ohio, in 1817. The timbers for the frame have been hewed from logs by hand. Pens held livestock while a central area provided space for threshing and storing grain. *Courtesy of Donald Hutslar.*

not meet the practical needs of farmers, particularly for the easy storage of hay and fodder, and because they were labor-intensive and expensive to build. In regard to specially designed barns such as these, then, the historian should ask where the farmer got his ideas for that distinctive style, whether there are regional variations, and which farmers were most likely to build them.

In the Midwest, a three-portal barn, which is a form of the crib barn, became popular. It has three doors and aisles with pens and cribs on each side that run the length of the barn. German settlers may have introduced this architectural style to the Midwest, because it can be found in the Lower Saxony, Westfalen-Lippe, and Mecklenburg areas of Europe. The three-portal barn is often called a feeder barn because farmers primarily used them to shelter livestock. This barn became the standard style in the Midwest during the late nineteenth and early twentieth centuries. During the twentieth century the three-portal barn began to rival the great ethnically derived barns in size as farmers used them to house livestock, grain, hay, and farm machinery.

In many areas the metal pole barn became popular after World War II. This barn consists of poles or beams that serve as the structure for the attachment of the walls. In contrast to other barn styles, the pole barn does not reflect ethnic settlement patterns or architectural traditions. These metal structures are cheaper to build and maintain than traditional wooden barns. Because many farmers had adopted the silo,

Crib barns stored fodder or sheltered livestock. These modest log structures often have vertical siding and additions that conceal the original building. *Courtesy of the Ohio Historical Society.*

when these barns became popular, the structure did not require a hay-loft. Consequently, the pole barn is a one-story structure. Because the siding can be attached to the poles or beams that have been embedded in concrete, the barn does not need a foundation. The large open area within the barn can be divided into various useable spaces, or the pole barn can serve as a large garage for power equipment, such as tractors, combines, and cotton pickers. By the late twentieth century, metal pole barns had spread across the countryside, bringing a homogenization of architectural barn styles to rural America.

Barn styles, then, can tell a great deal about ethnicity, immigration, and agricultural development. In the area known as Paddy's Run near Cincinnati, Ohio, for example, Welsh farmers first settled the land and built English barns. Today, those farmsteads remain occupied by fami-

Octagonal barns became popular during the late nineteenth century in the Midwest. This octagonal barn in Iowa dates from the 1920s. It had a hayloft from which forage could be pitched down to livestock in the stalls along the walls. *Photo courtesy State Historical Society of Iowa—Des Moines.*

lies with British surnames. In contrast, the Swiss Mennonites, who settled fewer than ten miles east of the Welsh during the 1830s, built massive two-story bank barns with gable roofs. African Americans, who settled nearby in Carthagena during the last half of the nineteenth century, brought a southern architectural barn style with them as they migrated north. The barns of these black farmers resembled the tobacco barns from the Tidewater South with their small size and unpainted, vertical siding with air spaces between the boards. The roofs have steep pitches, the doors have overhangs, and sheds are often attached to three sides.

Some barn styles are specific to particular regions. The connected barn, for example, is found almost entirely in New England. It is a barn attached to the house enabling the farm family to live at one end

Round barns had a silo in the center to enable easy feeding of livestock. Unfortunately, the labor required to fill it proved an inefficient use of time, and few farmers built them after the 1920s. *Photo courtesy State Historical Society of Iowa—Des Moines.*

and the livestock to be sheltered at the other with intervening storage and work rooms. This connected structure enabled movement from the house to the barn during the winter without going outside. It also indicates attempts to organize agricultural production and home industries as well as the influence of connected townhouses in New England's cities. These barns became popular in the mid-nineteenth century in prosperous and increasingly commercial agricultural areas where the English population lived in relative isolation from other ethnic groups.

Similarly, specialty barns indicate specific needs of farmers. Tobacco barns are characteristically built only in the areas where the leaf is grown. The style depends on whether the tobacco is to be air-, fire- or flue-cured. In North Carolina, flue-cured tobacco barns have shed roofs, much like the roofs over a porch. These roofs skirt the building

Traverse tobacco barns are designed to air-cure tobacco. Louvers on the sides open to permit air circulation among the leaves which hang from racks. Sometimes these tobacco barns have an attached stripping shed. *Courtesy of the Ohio Historical Society.*

and can be identified in at least fourteen styles, each designed to meet the stripping, curing, and warehouse needs of the farmer. Where the crop is cured by unheated air, tobacco barns have hinged shutters or louvers along the walls that can be opened to provide ventilation. These louvers open either vertically or horizontally. When farmers air-cure their tobacco, they leave the louvers open at all times except during rainy or damp weather. If the weather is exceptionally dry, however, the louvers are opened only at night to prevent the leaves from curing too quickly. The tobacco hangs from racks or horizontal laths or rods. Tobacco barns usually have at least one set of doors large enough to permit the entry of a wagon. Windows are located only at one end of the barn. If a stripping room is located beneath the floor, it usually has several windows. There, workers prepared the cured leaves for sale.

In other areas localized architecture gives a distinctive appearance to barns, such as the gambrel-roofed, multipurpose barns with off-center side doors seen along the Lake Erie shore. Although also found in Maine, West Virginia, and on the fringe of the Chesapeake Bay, this barn apparently does not have any ethnic history. The farm historian should not be overly concerned if he or she is unable to precisely determine ethnic influences or identify a barn style, because combinations of several designs or modifications frequently occurred to meet specific needs, or, because the farmers adopted a particular architectural fad, such as round barns, even though those barns did not entirely meet their needs. Certainly, the historian should remember that barn architecture can show regional concentration that indicates cultural diffusion and ethnic settlement patterns as well as agricultural emphasis, such as specific crops or livestock raising. But, the architecture may only indicate the preferences of the builder who worked in a free-lance fashion without regard to tradition. Indeed, the farm historian must remember that many barn styles cannot be categorized because they are a homogenization of styles or a style that emerged from the architectural skills of an independent farmer-builder who worked with the available and affordable materials to meet his specific needs.

At the same time, the farm historian should not worry if he or she cannot precisely date the barn. Exact dating is difficult if not impossible, unless the historian has a written record, such as an account book or letter. Without such documentation, however, an investigator can make an educated guess. One should look for vertical saw marks which indicate a pre-Civil War building. If the siding has been attached with cut nails, the dating is post-1800, while round nails mean twentieth-century construction. Barns with sawed lath for walls date since 1850. Barns also may have various additions over time, which make the dating of the barn difficult. Usually, researchers will only be able to give an approximate date based on their knowledge of settlement patterns in the area.

Barn styles may also tell a historian, particularly one who does not live in the area, much about environmental conditions. Hayhoods attached to barns in Appalachia indicate the need to store hay during the summer when shade is important to the individuals pitching from the wagon to the loft. The saltbox design indicates the desire to use heavy snowfall as an insulating sheath because it will envelop the roof and eave thereby keeping the inside warm for the livestock. Other barn styles may indicate considerations for wind direction and the angle of the sun's rays during both summer and winter.

Although barn styles reflect culture, the historian should remember that American farmers have always been a practical, utilitarian people. In that regard, barn styles were not usually adopted merely because of tradition, but rather to meet specific needs. Farmers customarily made modifications over the decades. The development of silos and haybalers, for example, made haylofts unnecessary, because forage could be stored outside the barn. In addition, if a silo is attached or located be-

Many barns are combinations of a specific style and layout to meet a farmer's needs. This barn was built near Amana, Iowa, about 1890. It has a forebay reminiscent of the German Sweitzer barn, but it is especially designed to hold a considerable amount of hay in the loft and cattle, probably for milking, in the stalls below. *Photo courtesy State Historical Society of Iowa—Des Moines.*

side the barn, it was built after 1875, when farmers became more knowledgeable about fermentation as a preservative for forage crops. The silo also may indicate a shift in farm emphasis for the production of cattle for beef or dairy purposes. Farm account books, diaries, or local newspapers may help confirm economic changes in the neighborhood. Usually, shifting emphasis in production meant constructing a new barn if the old one could not be remodeled easily. Barns, then, are cultural artifacts. By reading their design, construction, and alterations, the historian can learn much about the agricultural history of the farm.

OTHER FARM BUILDINGS

The historian should pay close attention to the other buildings on the farm. Was there or is there a springhouse? These buildings would have been located in a low area where springwater flowed with sufficient volume for household use and to cool pans of milk, butter, fruits, and vegetables. The water flowed through stone or concrete channels where pans, crocks, and jugs were set for their contents to cool. If the springhouse has an upper level large enough to be a living space, then the farmer probably employed a hired man who lived there. If no records of such employment can found, this level may have been used for churning butter and pressing cheese. If the springhouse had two rooms, the larger room probably was used for separating cream and making butter. If that room had a fireplace, the farm wife probably used it for a laundry, a place to make soap and apple butter, or as an area for processing meat from freshly slaughtered hogs. If the historian has located a small house which is entered by descending steps, with only a few small windows, or none at all, if the floor is paved with stones or bricks, if boxlike openings were built in the walls, or if stones protruded for storage or shelving, he or she probably has found a springhouse. The existence of a springhouse meant the farm women had another task on the farm—keeping it cleaned and whitewashed.

Small, one-room houses with a fireplace, such as those commonly found in the Great Valley and among the German settlers in Pennsylvania indicate a summer kitchen or house. These buildings were used for the preparation of food in the summer to help keep the main house cool. They also served as a place to preserve fruit and vegetables from spring to autumn. In time, summer kitchens often became incorporated into the main farmhouse and thereby lost their unique importance to agricultural life.

Similarly, smokehouses, usually located near the farmhouse, indicate that, prior to the age of mechanical refrigeration, the family raised livestock at least to meet their own food needs. Smokehouses usually extended from six to eight feet on the sides and from eight to twelve feet high. Vents let the smoke out at the eaves and through the roof while the fire pit occupied the center of the building. The farm historian must be careful not to mislabel these small vertical structures as privies.

Sometimes smokehouses also served as bakeovens. When bakeovens stood alone, however, they were located close to the kitchen. Farmers built these ovens from wood, brick, or stone, and the dimensions extended about twelve feet long, and eight feet wide and high. Overhanging eaves provided protection for cooling bread and pies and for hanging utensils. The floors of the bakeovens usually had an opening through which the wood ashes could be dropped into the ash pit below. Bakeovens had a door or opening on one end and an oven with an iron door and chimney on the other. Today, remaining bakeovens usually serve as storage sheds for lawn and garden tools.

Icehouses also existed on many farms before the age of refrigeration. Often they were built with stone walls below ground. Above ground icehouses were built from hardwood boards. The best ice-

Springhouses were used to cool milk, butter, and other perishable foods in a pre-refrigeration age. Water entered the building and ran through troughs crafted from stone in the floor. *Courtesy of Donald Hutslar.*

house had double walls below ground with two feet of sawdust or straw placed between the partitions to provide insulation. The earth or sand floors absorbed the water from melting ice. A vent at the top and bottom allowed hot air to escape. A double door, preferably on the north side, provided access. If the farm historian discovers a building such as this with dimensions of twelve to fourteen feet square, it probably was an icehouse.

In fruit growing areas small dryhouses usually were located near the kitchen. Often these structures were portable, although some were built from brick or stone. Dryhouses usually measured only four by six feet. These houses enabled farm women to preserve large quantities of fruits and vegetables without heating the kitchen. Rows of horizontal trays held the fruits and vegetables which dried from the heat of a stove. Sometimes bakeovens also served as dryhouses.

Sugarhouses sometimes can be found on farms from New England to Ohio. The farm family brought the sap, which they had collected from maple trees, called a sugar bush, to these buildings for processing into a useable and saleable product. Sugarhouses varied in size, but each usually included a room for the evaporator, which converted the sap to syrup, as well as storage and packing areas. A standard design during the late nineteenth and early twentieth centuries called for a building sixteen by thirty-six feet, and twelve feet high. Sometimes, sugarhouses were built on the side of a hill so the sap could be easily transferred from the gathering wagon or sled to the storage tanks without pumping or handling.

Most farmsteads also had a cellar for storing preserved fruits and vegetables or root crops such as potatoes, yams, and turnips. If no springs existed on the farm, the cellar proved an important substitute for a springhouse. The farm historian should look for cellar openings, usually double wooden doors leading to an underground pit or into a nearby hillside. Where bank barns remain, the researcher should look for cellars beneath the ramp leading to the middle floor. Farmers customarily built cellar walls from stone or brick and covered the top with several feet of earth for insulation. Ventilation ducts enabled the circulation of the air. If properly ventilated these cellars created a cool, dry storage area during the summer and prevented foods from freezing during the winter, with the temperature holding at approximately sixty degrees throughout the year. In some areas of the Midwest and Great Plains, farm cellars served as a place of refuge during storms that had the potential of generating tornadoes.

The historian also should locate the privy or at least determine where it was situated. These structures can be easily confused with smokehouses from a distance, but on close inspection they are easy to identify because they measure only about five to seven feet on a side and seven to ten feet high, with an inside platform with one or two holes in it. Usually, the door had a symbol, such as a crescent, star, or diamond, cut through at the top or on the sides to provide ventilation and light. If one seat is located lower than the other, it indicates that children lived on the farm before the age of electricity, pumps, and indoor plumbing.

In addition, the researcher should look for wood and wagon sheds and carriage houses. Wagon sheds often served as multipurpose buildings with storage cribs for corn, a hayloft, workbench, and forge. Often wagon sheds were built against the barn wall or close to it. Carriage houses usually were lean-to buildings attached to the wagon shed. On prosperous farms the carriage house could be found between the barn and the kitchen, and it had more substantial construction than the wagon house. In time farmers often converted carriage houses into garages for their cars, trucks, and tractors as well as other equipment. Sometimes these structures were also converted into chicken houses and pigpens.

Buildings that have several inches of space between the siding were used as corn cribs. An opening is located near the roof or on the sides for receiving the corn that remained on the cob. The space between the siding permitted air circulation and helped dry the corn. The floors of these cribs are above ground level to enhance circulation and discourage pests. The number and size of the corn cribs on a farm helps indicate the fertility of the soil, scale of operation, and crop emphasis.

The historian will, no doubt, discover other buildings on the farm which are no longer in use or are used for purposes other than their original intent. Pigpens and chicken houses provide good examples of structures that may no longer be used to house swine and poultry because the farm family does not find it economically viable to do so today. Pigpens usually were located on well drained land, down wind from the farmhouse. Farmers preferred to face the pigpens toward the south or east to enhance winter shelter. Pigpens rose about ten or twelve feet high in front and sloped to six or eight feet at the eaves in the rear. Inside, the pens extended from five to eight feet wide and about ten feet long. Usually the floors were of earth or sometimes stone, with one window per pen providing light and ventilation. Where farmers depended on hogs for commercial production, rather than subsistence, the pens tended to be much larger. Chicken houses were also built to take advantage of drainage and sunlight. Often they have a flat, sloping roof with roosts and nests well placed to avoid drafts.

The historian should also look for a milkhouse and a pumphouse, which often were one building. Milkhouses became popular during the late nineteenth and early twentieth centuries as fluid milk consumption and production increased. The milkhouse replaced the springhouse for cooling milk, cream, and butter. Milkhouses often were built near or over a spring, well or icehouse, although sometimes they were attached to the barn. (Occasionally, however, farmers who milked only one or two cows to meet family needs had a special room in the barn for separating the milk and cream and storing the cans in a tank of cool water.) Milkhouses measured about twelve feet long and eight feet wide. They were constructed from wood, tile, bricks, stone, or concrete blocks. A drain allowed spilled milk to escape and the floor to be washed. The cement or plaster walls, painted white, gave the milkhouse a clean, well-lighted appearance. A pump or windmill brought water to the tanks. The milkhouse had a separator and a trough to hold the milk and cream cans for cooling. The pumphouse sometimes served as a milkhouse, but farm women usually used it for laundry. In such a case the pumphouse would likely be located near the kitchen door.

FARMHOUSES

In addition to exploring the architectural story of the barnyard, the historian would also be wise to investigate the history of the farmhouse. Farmhouses tell much about the agricultural age in which they were built. Indeed, farmhouses usually have been designed for practicality and function rather than for style or ostentation. Between 1830 and 1900 in the northern United States, for example, agricultural journals often discussed design and layout to improve the efficiency of the farm home and enhance domestic affairs. Prior to the 1850s, for instance, designers placed the kitchen at the back of the house to facilitate access to the barn or garden, located a nursery close to the kitchen, and provided a room for the hired hand.

Until the mid-nineteenth century farm women were valued for their contribution to the production of the farm as well as their roles as wives and mothers within the farm home. Caring for poultry, tending the garden, preserving fruits, canning vegetables, and making butter as well as raising children, cooking, sewing, and cleaning meant that life in the farm home and farmyard overlapped and the house had to meet a variety of daily work requirements. Between 1855 and 1885, however, mechanization and access to urban markets promoted agricultural specialization, particularly for dairying and fruit and vegetable production in the North, and men assumed many of the tasks previously relegated to women. As a result, the role of farm women began to change from actively assisting with labor in the barns and fields to working in the home, that is, the domestic sphere of the farm. The farmhouse underwent corresponding architectural specialization. The kitchen, for example, became less a place to process foods for market than to prepare food for the family. The home became less a place for merely sleeping and more a domain for raising children. As a result, the layout of the farm home began to change among "progressive" farm families.

Indeed, during the late nineteenth century unified work space in the farm home gave way to specialized and isolated rooms. With cream and milk now being taken to urban creameries for pasteurization and processing into butter, the kitchen of the farm home did not require easy and direct access to the barn. Kitchens now began to be built in the front of the house facing the public roadway and where the sun provided light and a comfortable feeling for the women who spent most of their time there. This location also suggested that farm women now looked beyond their gate for social contact. The nursery or playroom for the children also moved away from the kitchen, and, as mechanization eliminated the need for hired workers, rooms for farmhands were converted to other purposes. As a result, the rooms of the farm home became increasingly divided between work and family and more individualized and less communal, although many designers maintained the integrity of the informal sitting or living room instead of including the more formal and urban parlor in their construction plans.

Moreover, between 1880 and 1900, designers of northern farm homes began to provide separate bedrooms for children, a feature that indicated the increasing importance of children in American rural society. Single rooms offered at least some autonomy and the opportunity for some individualism. These designs also indicate that families were becoming smaller and aspiring to higher standards of living. Certainly, by the twentieth century progressive farm homes in the northern United States reflected the design priorities of family life rather than agricultural production. Family activities, such as preparing and serving food, informal visiting, and sleeping, began to dominate architectural design. The results were fewer rooms, smaller kitchens, informal living rooms, and more isolated, private, and age-segregated bedrooms, while formal parlors, sleeping rooms for hired hands, and large, multipurpose kitchens began to disappear from new farm homes.

Historians, then, should look for indications that the layout of the farm home reflected the need for family cooperation and communal work as well as whether it provided privacy and recreational opportunities. The researcher might also ask whether the design reflected changing mechanization and specialization and the decreased need for women, children, and hired hands to help with the farm work. Simply put, the historian ought to think about the arrangement of the domestic space in the home in relation to farm life. Certainly, the historian will want to identify a formal style, such as Greek, Georgian, or Gothic, or vernacular types, such as the I, T, single pen, stack, or saddlebag house, and whether the house is built from brick or wood. But, thoughtful researchers do more than merely identify architectural style, they analyze the arrangement of space in relation to the farm

The historian can learn much about work patterns and social interaction on the farm by studying its architecture, particularly the house. This organized space is an important part of the farm's history. *Courtesy of United States Department of Agriculture.*

and the people who have lived there. Space affected the daily lives of the men, women, and children who have lived in the farmhouse.

Agricultural magazines and newspapers will show the local historian the kinds of designs that contemporaries considered "progressive." Not all farm families built homes based on these designs or even remodeled their houses to meet changing needs or tastes. Still, many families altered their homes over time to meet new agricultural and domestic conditions, and the farm historian should be aware of these alterations. Where progressive designs were adopted, the farm family served as a cultural arbitrator; they were making choices between the urban and rural worlds. They had the means to build more expensive and formally designed houses as well as knowledge of changing architectural styles based on both form and function. Other farm families also adopted bits and pieces of new designs to meet their particularly needs and financial conditions.

Although these examples of changes in farm homes among progressive farmers in the northern United States will not necessarily correspond to architectural designs and changes in other regions, they suggest the kinds of questions historians need to ask about the home when exploring the farm's past. It is important to investigate when the farm home was built and by whom. But, it is just as important to consider why it was built in that particular manner, and why specific alterations have been made over the years. No matter whether the historian is examining the history of a plantation mansion in the South, a ranch house in the Southwest, or a farm home in the Pacific Northwest, the story will not be complete without inclusion of the architectural history of the house. Historians seeking to pursue the history of architecture and social developments in relation to family homes should begin with Barbara J. Howe et al., *Houses and Homes: Exploring Their History* (Nashville: American Association for State and Local History, 1987).

GARDENS

No history of the farm will be complete without an investigation of the vegetable, fruit, and flower gardens around the home. The historian should attempt to determine the varieties of fruits, vegetables, and flowers that have been raised on the farm over time. Sometimes, gardens have always been located in one place, but the historian may find evidence that the locations of the gardens have changed, and the researcher will do well to sketch those sites. Oral histories, diaries, letters, and even recipes can provide information about the locations of gardens and the plants raised. Still, the identification of specific varieties can prove difficult, because plants leave little evidence beyond their seeds, and many varieties often had various names in different regions. Contemporary agricultural and horticultural magazines and journals, such as the *New England Farmer, Ohio Cultivator, Western Farmer and Gardener, American Gardener's Magazine,* and *Gardener's Monthly* as well as seed catalogs, premium lists for county and state fairs, and photographs will help the farm historian identify those varieties or at least enable her or him to make an educated guess. Specialists at nearby living historical farms may be able to help identify varieties, and seed companies may have selected antique varieties. Garden clubs, seed exchanges, and heirloom gardeners will also be able to provide information or access to various seeds. The thorough historian also will wish to ask the family or families who have operated the farm or nearby farm families whether they can identify the varieties of fruits and vegetables grown and whether they have any seeds that the researcher might plant. This requires, of course, that the historian live in an area where those varieties can be raised.

Still, the farm historian must remember that gaining hard evidence about gardens often proves elusive and that approximations about the varieties of fruits and vegetables grown will usually be the best that can be determined. While some vegetable seeds have been passed from one generation to another and remain cultivated today, not all varieties raised in an Indiana farmer's garden in 1860 still exist. Many old varieties, commonly known as "heirlooms," have been replaced by more productive "improved" varieties, such as hybrids, and some have become extinct. Even so, the historian can learn much about farm production, daily foodways, and agricultural life by investigating the history of farm gardens. Moreover, one of the rewards of such research is that the historian can also raise some of those varieties. He or she can actually see and taste what the farm families of long ago consumed at their dinner tables, such as Black Spanish watermelons, Early Bush Scallop squash, and White Silesian lettuce.

Research on flower gardens can be equally difficult. Flower gardens, of course, change over time and the researcher will do best to investigate a specific time period, such as the 1860s, 1890s, or 1920s. The first task is to determine the flowers that were cultivated at a particular time. Then, the list can be narrowed to the flower varieties available through nurseries, peddlers, and mail order services. Last, the researcher can identify the flowers that were popular. The greatest difficulty involves identifying varieties of a specific flower, such as

Gardens have always been important for most farmers to help meet the food needs of the family as well as to sell to grocers in town or at roadside stands. The local historian should not overlook the garden in any study of the farm's history, because it will tell much about daily life—nutritionally, economically, and socially. This farm woman and her son are picking peas in their garden near Champion Valley, Nebraska, on July 2, 1925. *Courtesy of the Nebraska State Historical Society.*

peonies, daffodils, or tulips. "Origination lists" or "cumulative check lists" contain all known varieties of a flower as well as dates of introduction and a brief description. A variety of published origination lists can be found in Scott G. Kunst and Arthur O. Tucker, " 'Where Have All the Flowers Gone?' A Preliminary List of Origination Lists for Ornamental Plants," *APT Bulletin* 21, no. 2 (1989): 43–50. Contemporary newspapers and agricultural, horticultural, and nursery catalogs may also prove helpful.

Once the proper varieties have been identified, the researcher can also grow them for their enlightenment and aesthetic pleasure. By so doing, the history of farm gardens provide a "useable past" in a fashion that goes beyond the study of history to gain insight about the present.

SUGGESTED READINGS

Good introductory bibliographies that include contemporary and historical citations for farm structures are Howard Wight Marshall, *American Folk Architecture: A Selected Bibliography* (Washington, DC: Library of Congress, American Folklife Center Publications, 1981); Donald H. Dyal, *An International Bibliography of the Architecture of Agriculture* (Monticello, IL: Vance Bibliographies, 1982); Alvar W. Carlson, "Bibliography on Barns in the United States and Canada," *Pioneer America* 10, no. 1 (1978): 65–71; and Charles F. Calkins, *The Barn as an Element in the Cultural Landscape of North America: A Bibliography* (Monticello, IL: Vance Bibliographies, 1979). More detailed and well-illustrated studies that will be exceptionally helpful for the local historian who is attempting to identify barn styles include Allen G. Nobel *Wood, Brick, and Stone: The North American Settlement Landscape*, Vol. 2: *Barns and Farm Structures* (Amherst: University of Massachusetts Press, 1984). This study provides excellent bibliographical references in the end notes of each chapter. Similarly see, Stanley Schuler, *American Barns: In a Class By Themselves* (Exton, PA: Schiffer Pub. Ltd., 1984); Allen G. Noble and Gayle A. Seymour, "Distribution of Barn Types in Northeastern United States," *Geographical Review* 72 (April 1982): 155–70; and Allen G. Noble, "Barns as Elements in the Settlement Landscape of Ohio," *Pioneer America* 9 (January 1977): 62–79. See also Charles Klamkin, *Barns: Their History, Preservation, and Restoration* (New York: Hawthorne Books, 1973); Lawrence Grow, *Country Architecture: Old Fashioned Designs for Gazebos, Summerhouses, Springhouses, Smokehouses, Stables, Greenhouses, Carriage Houses, Outhouses, Icehouses.* . . . (Pittstown, NJ: Main Street Press, 1985); and Eric Arthur and Dudley Whitney, *The Barn* (New York: New York Geographic Society, 1972).

Eric Sloane emphasizes New England barns with excellent drawings in *American Barns & Covered Bridges* (New York: Funk and Wagnalls, 1954) and his study *An Age of Barns* (New York: Funk and Wagnalls, n.d.) includes similar drawings of barn styles from other regions. See also Thomas C. Hubka, *Big House, Little House, Back House, Barn: The Connected Farm Buildings of New England* (Hanover, NH: University Press of New England, 1984) and Wolbur Zelinsky, "The New England Connecting Barn," *Geographical Review* 48, no. 3 (October 1958): 540–53. Other specialized studies include, Robert F. Ensminger, *The Pennsylvania Barn: Its Origin, Evolution, and Distribution in North America* (Baltimore: Johns Hopkins University Press, 1992); Marian

Moffett and Lawrence Wodehouse, *East Tennessee Cantilever Barns* (Knoxville: University of Tennessee Press, 1993); and Vincent J. Schaefer, *Dutch Barns of New York: An Introduction* (Fleischmanns, NY: Purple Mountain Press, 1994). Schaefer's study provides an excellent glossary of barn terms as well as drawings and pictures of Dutch barn construction, but the standard authority on Dutch barns is John Fitchen, *The New World Dutch Barn: A Study of Its Characteristics, Its Structural System, and Its Probable Erectional Procedures* (Syracuse: Syracuse University Press, 1968). Two excellent studies of other specialty barns include John T. Hanou, *A Round Indiana: Round Barns in the Hoosier State* (West Lafayette: Purdue University Press, 1993) and Lowell J. Soike, *Without Right Angles: The Round Barns of Iowa* (Des Moines: Iowa State Historical Department, 1983). See also Henry Glassie, "The Barns of Appalachia," *Mountain Life and Work* 40 (Summer 1965): 21–30.

The cultural linkages to farm architecture is clearly apparent in Donald A. Hutslar, "The Ohio Farmstead: Farm Buildings as Cultural Artifacts," *Ohio History* 90 (Summer 1981): 221–37 and Stewart G. McHenry, "Vermont Barns: A Cultural Landscape Analysis," *Vermont History* 46 (Summer 1978): 151–56. See also Richard Francaviglia, "Western American Barns: Architectural Form and Climatic Considerations," *Yearbook of the Association of Pacific Coast Geographers* 34 (1972): 153–60. Allen G. Noble and Hubert G. H. Wilhelm have edited an important collection of essays entitled *Barns of the Midwest* (Athens: Ohio University Press, 1995). For an excellent brief description of many types of farm buildings found in the northern United States consult Amos Long, Jr., *Farmsteads and Their Buildings* (Lebanon, PA: Applied Art Publishers, 1976). See also Lewis F. Allen, *Rural Architecture* (New York: Orange Judd & Co., 1852).

Related architectural studies include two works by Allen G. Noble, "Barns and Square Silos in Northeast Ohio," *Pioneer America* 6 (July 1974): 12–21; "The Silo in the Eastern Midwest: Patterns of Evolution and Distribution," *Ohio Geographer* 4 (1976): 20–29; and Arn Henderson and Thomas D. Isern, "Wooden Silos of the Southern Great Plains," *Pioneer America Society Transactions* 8 (1985): 1–19. A brief overview of barn, home, and silo styles can be found in Wallace Ashby, "Fifty Years of Development in Farm Buildings," *Agricultural Engineering* 38 (June 1957): 426–32, 459.

Sally Ann McMurry provides an excellent analysis of the changing styles of farm homes among self-styled progressive farmers in the northern United States from 1830 to 1900 in *Families and Farmhouses in Nineteenth-Century America: Vernacular Design and Social Change* (New York: Oxford University Press, 1988). See also, Allen G. Noble, *Wood,*

Brick, and Stone: The North American Settlement Landscape, Vol. 1: *Houses* (Amherst: University of Massachusetts Press, 1984). More specialized studies include Howard Wight Marshall, *Folk Architecture in Little Dixie: A Regional Culture in Missouri* (Columbia: University of Missouri Press, 1981); Fred W. Peterson, "Vernacular Building and Victorian Architecture: Midwestern American Farm Homes," *Journal of Interdisciplinary History* 12 (Winter 1982): 409–27; Bernard Herman, *Architecture and Rural Life in Central Delaware, 1700–1900* (Knoxville: University of Tennessee Press, 1987); and John B. Jackson, *Discovering the Vernacular Landscape* (New Haven: Yale University Press, 1984).

Log houses and barns can still be found on some farms. For an introduction to identifying these structures and the techniques used to build them see C. A. Weslager, *The Log Cabin in America: From Pioneer Days to the Present* (New Brunswick: Rutgers University Press, 1969); Donald A. Hutslar, *The Architecture of Migration: Log Construction in the Ohio Country, 1750–1850* (Athens: Ohio University Press, 1986); and E. Duane Elbert and Keith A. Sculle, "Log Buildings in Illinois, Their Interpretation and Preservation," *Illinois Preservation Series no. 3* (Springfield: Illinois Department of Conservation, Division of Historic Sites, 1982). Terry G. Jordan has written two excellent studies that emphasize the cultural importance of log architecture, *Texas Log Buildings* (Austin: University of Texas Press, 1978) and *The American Backwoods Frontier: An Ethnic and Ecological Interpretation* (Baltimore: Johns Hopkins University Press, 1989). See also Matti Kaups, "Log Architecture in America: European Antecedents in a Finnish Context," *Journal of Cultural Geography* 2, no. 1 (1981): 131–53.

The local historian should consult Carolyn Jabs, *The Heirloom Gardener* (San Francisco: Sierra Club Books, 1984) for an introduction to collecting seed varieties from long ago. This study also includes a helpful list of seed exchanges and seed companies that maintain inventories of heirloom varieties. See also Robert Becker, Lynne Belluscio, and Roger Kline, *The Heirloom Vegetable Garden* (Ithaca, NY: Cornell University Cooperative Extension, n.d.) and Ulysses P. Hedrick, *A History of Horticulture in America to 1860* (New York: Oxford University Press, 1950).

Chapter 7

RESEARCH AND WRITING

Good research and writing require skills that historians gain and improve over time. Both require thought, planning, and work. Although it is too much to say that practice makes perfect because the historian is dealing with the uncertainties of the human condition, it is not to much to say that the more research and writing that historians do the better they get.

Most historians find that research is an ongoing process. Few complete all of their research before writing. Certainly, historians try to be as thorough with their research as possible before writing, but most find that even when they reach the writing stage, they will necessarily need to check other sources for matters of fact or clarification. Remember, however, perfectionists never accomplish anything because they are never finished with their work. At some point the historian must determine that he or she has enough material to begin writing, knowing full well that additional research will probably be necessary to fill in gaps or to clarify a particular topic.

Before a historian begins to write the history of a farm, however, it would be good to reflect on the sources consulted to make sure that the research has been comprehensive. The following outline is intended to be suggestive. Indeed, the farm historian will, no doubt, think of other research topics and sources. If, however, a major subject or source from the following list has not been pursued, the researcher probably should examine it for before beginning to write. The major research materials to consider are as follows:

I. Family sources
   A. Reminiscences (written and oral)
   B. Letters
   C. Diaries

    D. Account books
    E. Family Bibles
    F. Photograph albums
    G. Documents related to land ownership
    H. Church records
    I. School records
    J. Technology (implements, tools, household appliances, hybrid seed, fertilizers, pesticides)
    K. Architecture (barns, houses, outbuildings)
    L. Wills
II. Local Community Sources
    A. Newspapers
    B. Deeds [Register of Deeds]
    C. Probate Court records
    D. Naturalization records [Clerk of the District Court and sometimes Federal Court]
    E. Files in local library
    F. Files at county and state historical societies
    G. County atlases, histories, and gazetteers
    I. Directories—city, county, telephone
    K. Books and articles published about the local area
III. Federal and State Sources
    A. Federal manuscript census schedules for 1850–1920
    B. State manuscript census schedules
    C. Publications of the state board of agriculture
    D. Publications of the state agricultural experiment station
    E. Public documents in the state archives
    F. Maps
IV. Oral History (with owners, operators, friends, and neighbors)
    A. Questions relating to family agricultural experiences
       1. Names of owners and operators (past and present)
       2. Nature of farm life
    B. Daily farm schedule for family members
       1. Organization of family work
       2. Leisure-time activities
       3. Organizational activities
       4. Decision making
       5. Schooling
       6. Religious activities
       7. Labor concerns
       8. Inheritance practices

C. National Affairs
   1. Effects of economic depressions
   2. Effects of wars
   3. Labor shortages or problems
   4. Government programs
   5. Technological change
   6. Social change

When considering these sources and subjects, the researcher will be wise to take notes. Note taking is valuable in any research project. No one can remember everything, and often the mind plays tricks with even the simplest information. Consequently, the historian profits from writing things down. Moreover, when it comes time to write the history of the farm, the researcher will find it useful to be able to organize the notes topically and chronologically in order to write with direction, purpose, and control.

Historians find that they save much time and avoid considerable irritation and frustration by adopting the best mechanical techniques for taking notes. Specifically, researchers have discovered that it is wise to resist the temptation to use notebooks. Notebooks are easy to use, and they enable the researcher to compile a considerable amount of information. Unfortunately, after the notes have been taken they are difficult to use because invariably the facts relating to many topics have been written on one page. As a result, the pages cannot be easily organized, and when notes are written on both sides of the page, they can become a nightmare to locate. Indeed, the use of notebooks is perhaps the worst possible method for taking notes.

Most historians have learned, often by trial and error, that the best mechanical system for taking notes is the use of note cards, either three by five, four by six, or five by eight inches. These cards along with filing boxes and alphabetical card dividers can be purchased at business office supply stores. College or university book stores also have these items. Even with note cards, however, a good axiom for taking notes is: "Never Write on the Back of Anything." This admonishment is easy to make and hard to follow. Both professional and amateur historians, however, quickly discover the wisdom of that axiom after they have lost important information on the back of a note card.

Note taking is a matter of personal preference, but the local historian will do well to use the five by eight cards, because they are easier to handle, and the researcher can write on them without cramping the words into a small space, as often happens when three by five cards are used. On each card the historian needs to write the name of the source at the top along with the author, title, volume number, and place of publication as well as the inclusive page numbers for books and articles. If the source is an unpublished record, the historian ought to provide as much information as possible, so that the history of the farm can be properly documented as well as to enable the researcher to return to that source easily for additional information.

Often, the researcher will need more than one card per source. Each card must have the necessary bibliographical citation at the top in order to keep those sources identifiable and enable proper organization, whether filed alphabetically or, preferably, by category. In addition, the researcher may find it useful to write a key word in an upper corner of the card to enable quick identification of the subject matter. This permits easy filing by topic and the later organization of the cards for writing. The following examples for citing a book and an article on an index card show how to record the essential bibliographic information:

Barns   Story County
Soike, Lowell J. *Without Right Angles: The Round Barns of Iowa.*
Des Moines: Iowa State Historical Department, 1983.

Technology   Tractors
Bogue, Allan G. "Changes in Mechanical and Plant Technol-
ogy: The Corn Belt, 1910–1940," *Journal of Economic History* 43
(March 1983): 1–25.

By using this procedure, note cards can be easily filed according to specific categories, such as farm life, organizations, New Deal farm programs, technological change, or daily life—1920s.

Researchers will save time later if they only take one note per card, that is, if they do not mix notes on technology, family life, economic conditions, and architecture. Becoming accustomed to this disciplined note taking is often difficult in the beginning, particularly if the researcher has considerable space left on the card after making the essential note, but combining notes should be resisted. Those who do not resist will have organizational problems with the notes during the writing stage. At the same time, the careful researcher will find it helpful also to record the page number for the noted information if it comes from a book or article, and the page and column number if from a newspaper.

Photocopies, like notebooks, pose organizational problems, although photocopying saves time, particularly with newspaper work. The historian may be best served by clipping the appropriate photocopied articles and gluing them to note cards for future reference and better organization and handling of the material.

Any note which is a direct, word-for-word copy from a book, manuscript, newspaper, or other source must be placed in quotation marks. Any note that is a paraphrase or summary should not be placed in quotation marks. The researcher must be careful when copying word for word. The note on the card must be identical to the passage, including spelling and punctuation. Do not use abbreviations that are not given in the original document and do not spell out abbreviations. If you leave out some words use ellipses, that is, three dots [. . .] to show that you have done so. If you add any words for clarification place them in brackets, not parentheses, to show that they are your own words. These techniques will save time and trouble later when the researcher has many note cards and cannot easily recall precisely whether the note was a verbatim passage or an extrapolation of the subject matter.

Careful research techniques will make the organizational and writing process easier. Except for direct quotations, however, the researcher has the personal freedom to use any technique that works best. Shorthand, abbreviations, even jargon, can work. The task at hand is to get the information transferred from the original document to a note card for later use. The only requirement is that the notes make sense to the researcher. Beyond the technical need to make correct bibliographic citations to permit the accurate documentation of the work and to enable the researcher to return to that source without difficulty, taking notes is a private and personal matter. The researcher usually takes notes only for him- or herself. Note cards cannot be used easily by anyone else. Historians must take their own notes, but they can do so in any manner that makes sense to them so long as the process ensures accuracy. When historians work in collaboration they should agree on a systematic method of note taking so that each researcher can easily use the notes taken by his or her colleague. The historian must remember, however, that he or she may not be ready to begin writing for several months or years, and the subject headings and legibility of the notes must make sense and be readable at a later date.

Once the historian has essentially completed the research for the history of a farm, it is time to read over his or her notes. If the notes cards have been filed by subject as the work progressed, the researcher will now have less work to do sorting them into appropriate categories. If not, the time has come to make organizational sense out of the notes by placing them in appropriate categories that will enable more specific sorting and organization. Prior to writing a history of the farm, one may wish, for instance, to place the card that notes the purchase of a wire binder before the note that records the acquisition of a self-propelled combine.

After the notes cards have been organized, it is time to write. A blank page can create a major hurdle, particularly if the researcher has not thought about the organizational structure of the farm's history. A good way to avoid the trepidation that can come from the sight of a blank page and stacks of note cards is to begin by writing an outline. Experienced historians first read through the notes, once again, for each particular subject. Then, the researcher ought to be able to organize his or her thoughts on paper in terms of the subject matter and chronology to be covered. Outlines help the historian to keep focused and to write in a logical, purposeful manner. Like note taking, outlines vary according to the idiosyncracies of the author. Some outlines may be long and detailed, while others brief and fragmented. In either case, any outline is better than no outline, and the farm historian's own organizational preferences will often work the best. Outlines, then, help the historian decide what to say and the order in which to say it. An outline, of course, takes time to prepare, but the expenditure of time is worth the effort, because it helps eliminate wasteful starts, meandering prose, and organizational chaos.

After the outline has been completed and the note cards arranged by subject, chronology, or some other organizational division, the best way to begin is by beginning. The historian need not worry about writing a first draft that is great historical literature. Rather, the goal should be to write clearly and directly. Matters of style will take care of themselves. It is important to remember that the hard part of writing is to get the idea from the brain onto the paper via a pen, typewriter, or computer. Once the essential ideas, that is, words, are on paper, the historian can revise. Indeed, the key to good writing is rewriting, but something must be written in the first place. So, historians should not agonize to the point of creating writer's block because their sentences seem awkward. The important matter at hand is to get the facts down clearly.

In order to write clearly and directly, however, the historian should consciously avoid stilted language, jargon, cliches, and colloquialisms. Writing is more formal than everyday spoken English, and historians should avoid writing in the fragmentary and vague manner of much casual speech. At the same time, the historian should avoid the flowery use of adjectives, or, as such writing is commonly known, "purple prose." Simply put, the historian should not try to embellish his or her writing or overly dramatize it. If the subject is dramatic, or at least important, clear, direct writing will convey the significance of the matter to the reader.

In addition, the writer should make every effort to avoid the repetition of the same word or words as well as the use of similes and metaphors. Readers may be be put off by statements, for example, that: "The threshing machine roared like thunder," or that "The harvest crew worked like madmen before the oncoming storm." Simply write that the threshing machine "roared" and the work crew "hurried." At the same time, historians can add energy to their prose by using the active rather than the passive voice as much as possible. This means avoiding sentence constructions that use the verbs "was" and "were" as well as "by" when it is used as a preposition. For example: "Migrant workers harvested the lettuce crop" works better than "The lettuce crop was harvested by migrant workers." Sometimes, the passive voice will serve the writer best, but it should be used sparingly as should the unidentifiable "it" or "this." The result will be clean, vibrant prose.

At the same time that the farm historian is endeavoring to write clearly and directly, he or she must always write with a purpose. Certainly, the purpose is to tell the history of a particular farm, but it is more than mere storytelling. The thoughtful historian always strives to be aware of cause and effect as well as the significance of events over time and within the context of place. Moreover, in their concern for accuracy, they try not to stray from the known record, that is, the facts, as documented from a variety of sources on the note cards. Novelists make things up, but conscientious historians only go so far as the evidence permits. This does not mean that historians do not interpret the evidence. Indeed, all effective historians give interpretive meaning to their story. Otherwise their work is merely descriptive and as such, does not contribute much to understanding or enable new ways of viewing the past. Simply put, the facts mean something, but they usually do not stand alone or speak for themselves. Consequently, it is the historians' responsibility to give them shape and meaning, both for themselves and for whomever reads their work.

Outlines, word usage, and interpretation will not have the greatest effect on the narrative of the farm, however, unless the history has structure. The historian must make a conscious effort to divide the story into elements, sections, or chapters. Each should have an introduction (usually a solid paragraph), body, and conclusion or summary. The writer must get to the subject at hand on the first page. Introductions let them do so. They set the stage and give continuity to following chapters. The body or narrative of each section will be composed of paragraphs that should each have a topic sentence. Topic sentences do not always and should not always come at the beginning of a paragraph, but as a central statement of the paragraph's purpose they are essential. Topic sentences give transition between paragraphs and keep the reader focused on the subject and the progression of the story. The structure of the narrative, then, helps keep readers intellectually organized.

The farm historian must also be careful to write only about the subject at hand. Digressions, irrelevancies, or emphasis on matters not germane to the the topic under discussion must be avoided. Editing or rewriting will eliminate many of these problems, but the historian should guard against them during the writing process.

At the end of each element of the farm's history, the writer should craft a concluding paragraph that emphasizes the significance of the topic to the history of the farm. Or, the historian should write a summary paragraph which briefly reviews the major points just discussed. Whether the farm historian prefers to write conclusions or summaries, the key to each is to stress the significance of the subject matter examined in that section to the farm's history.

Serious historians also work to ensure that the history of the farm has a professional appearance, that is, proper spelling, capitalization, punctuation, quotation, and use of dates, numbers, and italics, and show methodological technique. This latter matter involves the proper documentation of the manuscript through the use of foot- or endnotes. Documentation means that the historian systematically notes the sources used when writing, such as oral histories, letters, account books, wills, and newspapers. Footnotes and endnotes are essentially the same form of documentation except they are located either at the bottom of the page or at the end of a chapter. If the history of the farm is to be typed, endnotes may be easier than calculating space at the end of each page for footnotes. Most computer word processing programs, however, automatically place the notes at the bottom of the page, thereby speeding this tedious task. Researchers should feel free to use the documenting technique that they prefer. The location of the notes is not important, but the documentation of the history is essential.

The history of the farm should be documented for two important reasons. First, it will show the reader the sources used to craft the narrative and enable other researchers to consult those sources that may be helpful to their own work. The source citations thereby contribute to the increase of knowledge. Second, the documentation enables other researchers to check the evidence to validate the reliability of the history. Simply put, history is not fiction. It is the documented record of past events. By showing the sources that they have used, historians ensure that their work will be judged to be credible. If the farm historian does not document his or her work, it may be questioned by anyone who reads it. The documentation invites readers to check facts for themselves. Thereafter, the interpretation of those facts may vary, but no one should question the factual accuracy of the history.

The researcher can purchase several style manuals from book stores. Among the best and easiest to use is Kate L. Turabian, *A Manual for Writers of Term Papers, Theses, and Dissertations* (Chicago: University of Chicago Press, 1987). This manual gives excellent examples of how to cite books, articles, newspapers, and unpublished sources as well as government records. For a useful general guide to grammar, documentation, and the mechanics of research and writing see Diana Hacker, *A Pocket Style Manual* (Boston: St. Martin's Press, 1993).

Creating documentary citations for a history is not difficult, but it requires attention to detail. Essentially, it involves placing a consecutive number after the sentence or passage that includes factual or interpretive material that is not common knowledge. If the citations within a paragraph threaten to get out of control, one number can be placed at the end of the paragraph and all sources used to write the paragraph included in one foot- or endnote. A citation should contain the name of the author, title of the book or article, volume number, publisher, city, date of publication, and the pages where the information was located. If several sources are used, the historian merely separates them in consecutive order with a semicolon.

The following examples show the use of books, articles, manuscripts, newpapers in one endnote:

1. Sally G. McMillen, *Black and White Women in the Old South* (Arlington, Heights, IL: Harlan Davidson, 1992), 25.

2. John C. Creighton, *A History of Columbia and Boone County* (Columbia, MO: Computer Graphics, 1987), 98; R. Douglas Hurt, "Planters and Slavery in Little Dixie," *Missouri Historical Review* 68 (July 1994): 406.

3. Nathaniel Leonard to Abiel Leonard, February 15, 1839, Abiel Leonard Papers, State Historical Society of Missouri, Columbia; *Boon's Lick Times* (Fayette), July 18, 1846.

If the history of the farm extends over several chapters, the foot- or endnote numbers begin anew with each chapter. At the end of the history, the farm historian should then list all of the sources used to write the manuscript in a bibliography. This is accomplished by collecting all of the books, articles, newspapers, manuscript collections, and government documents in separate sections and listing them in alphabetical order and in correct bibliographic form.

In summary, then, no matter whether the history of the farm is 5 or 50 pages in length, the farm historian will do well to begin at the earliest date possible and go to the present or some sensible point of time for the conclusion. In writing the history of the farm, which may be a family farm, a farm that a family once owned, or a farm of some importance or interest, the investigator is likely to find the greatest satisfaction in being as thorough in his or her research as possible. Moreover, historians will find it most rewarding to write with a purpose, that is, not merely record facts but give them meaning. Put differently, the historian's greatest challenge and achievement lies in explaining what the facts mean, that is, in interpreting them.

Events off the farm influenced the lives of the people who lived there and the history of the farm itself. At the same time, the activities of the families on the farm likely contributed not only to the history of that place, but also the agriculture patterns and life of the neighborhood, the county, state, and nation. Consequently, the farm historian is wise always to look for cause and effect and to examine significance in his or her writing. The result will be a contribution to knowledge that will elevate the history of the farm from antiquarianism, that is, recording facts for their own sake without explanation and interpretation to a document that will help others understand how things have come to be as they are, the fundamental task of all historians. A thoroughly researched, carefully written history of a farm, one that places the farm and the people who have lived on it in the context of time and place and relates the history of that farm to the wider world, will be grass-roots history at its best. And, that history will stand the test of time.

SUGGESTED READINGS

David E. Kyvig and Myron A. Marty provide excellent tips for writing local history in *Nearby History: Exploring the Past around You* (Nashville: American Association for State and Local History, 1984). For other excellent guides to writing local history see David H. Russo, *Keepers of Our Past: Local Historical Writing in the United States, 1820s–1930s* (New York: Greenwood Press, 1988); James Mahoney, *Local History: A Guide for Research and Writing* (Washington, DC: National Education Association, 1981); Thomas E. Felt, *Researching, Writing, and Publishing Local History* (Nashville: American Association for State and Local History, 1976); Richard W. Hale, Jr., "Methods of Research for the Amateur Historian," American Association for State and Local History, *Technical Leaflet No. 21*, 1969. Although the guide is designed to help undergraduates write term papers, Sherman Kent's, *Writing History* (New York: Appleton Century Crofts, 1967) will be useful for the farm historian who needs help with the mechanics of documentation.

Although it does not deal with writing the history of a farm, historians will profit from two essays in Felix Gilbert and Stephen R. Graubard, eds., *Historical Studies Today* (New York: W. W. Norton, 1972). Those essays are by Pierre Goubert, entitled "Local History," pp. 300–14, and by Lawrence Stone, entitled "English and United States Local History," pp. 315–19. See also Kirk Jeffrey, *Writing a Community History: Some Suggestions for Grassroots Historians* (Chicago: Newberry Library, n.d.); Sam Bass Warner "Writing Local History: The Uses of Social Statistics," American Association for State and Local History, *Technical Leaflet No. 7*, 1970; and Dave Morley and Ken Worpole, eds., *The Republic of Letters: Working Class Writing and Local Publishing* (London: Comedia Publishing Group, 1982).

The farm historian should also consult Jacques Barzun and Henry F. Graff, *The Modern Researcher* (Fort Worth: Harcourt Brace Jovanovich, 1992), which includes an excellent bibliography on historical methods. For help on writing see Jacques Barzun, *Simple and Direct: A Rhetoric for Writers* (Chicago: University of Chicago Press, 1995); William Zinsser, *On Writing Well: An Informal Guide to Writing Nonfiction* (New York: HarperCollins, 1995); and William Strunk and E. B. White, *The Elements of Style* (New York: Macmillan, 1979).

Farm historians will also profit from reading Barbara W. Tuckman, *Practicing History: Selected Essays* (New York: Knopf, 1981).

APPENDIX
Historical Societies and Agencies

Alabama Department of
  Archives and History
624 Washington Avenue
Montgomery, Alabama 36130
205-832-6510

Alabama Historical Commission
725 Monroe Street
Montgomery, Alabama 36130
205-832-6621

Alaska Historical Commission
3221 Providence Avenue
Anchorage, Alaska 99504
907-274-6222

Alaska Historical Society
Box 10-355
Anchorage, Alaska 99511

Arizona State Department of
  Library, Archives, and Public
  Records
3rd Floor, State Capitol
Phoenix, Arizona 85007
602-255-3701

Arkansas Historical Association
History Department
12 Ozark Hall
University of Arkansas
Fayetteville, Arkansas 72701
501-575-3001

Arkansas History Commission
One Capitol Mall
Little Rock, Arkansas 72201
501-371-2141

California State Department of
  Parks and Recreation
Box 2390
Sacramento, California 95811
916-445-2358

Colorado Division of State
  Archives and Public Records
1313 Sherman Street
Denver, Colorado 80203
3030-866-2055

The State Historical Society of
  Colorado
1300 Broadway
Denver, Colorado 80203
303-866-2136

Connecticut Historical
  Commission
59 South Prospect Street
Hartford, Connecticut 06106
203-566-3005

The Connecticut Historical
  Society
1 Elizabeth Street
Hartford, Connecticut 06105
203-236-5621

Delaware Division of Historical
  and Cultural Affiars
Hall of Records
Dover, Delaware 19901
302-736-5314

Florida Division of Archives, His-
  tory, and Records Management
R. A. Gray Building
Pensacola and Bronough Streets
Tallahassee, Florida 32301
904-488-1480

Florida Historical Society
University of South Florida
  Library
Tampa, Florida 33620
813-974-2731

Georgia Department of Archives
  and History
330 Capitol Avenue, S.E.
Atlanta, Georgia 30334
404-656-2358

Hawaii State Archives
Iolani Palace Grounds
Honolulu, Hawaii 96813
808-548-2355

Hawaiian Historical Society
560 Kawaiahao Street
Honolulu, Hawaii 96813
808-537-6271

Idaho State Historical Society
610 North Julia Davis Drive
Boise, Idaho 83702
208-334-2120

Illinois State Historical Society
Old State Capitol
Springfield, Illinois 62706
217-782-4836

Indiana Historical Bureau
140 North Senate Avenue
Indianapolis, Indiana 46204
317-232-2537

Indiana Historical Society
315 West Ohio Street
Indianapolis, Indiana 46202
317-232-1882

Iowa Division of Historical
  Museum and Archives
East 12th and Grand Avenue
Des Moines, Iowa 50319
515-281-5111

Kansas State Historical Society
6428 Southwest 6th Avenue
Topeka, Kansas 66615
913-272-8681

Kentucky Historical Society
300 West Broadway, Box H
Frankfort, Kentucky 40601
502-564-3016

Louisiana State Museum
751 Charles Street
New Orleans, Louisiana 70116
504-581-4321

Louisiana Historical Society
600 Maritime Building
203 Carondelet Street
New Orleans, Louisiana 70130
504-588-9044

Maine State Museum
State House Complex
Augusta, Maine 04333
207-289-2301

Maryland Historical Society
201 West Monument Street
Baltimore, Maryland 21201
301-685-3750

Massachusetts Historical
  Commission
294 Washington Street
Boston, Massachusetts 02108
617-727-8470

Massachusetts Historical Society
1154 Boylston Street
Boston, Massachusetts 02215
617-536-1608

Historical Society of Michigan
2117 Washtenaw Avenue
Ann Arbor, Michigan 48104
313-769-1828

Minnesota Historical Society
345 Kellogg Blvd., West
St. Paul, Minnesota 55102
612-296-6126

Mississippi Department of
  Archives and History
100 South State Street
Jackson, Mississippi 39201
601-354-6218

State Historical Society of
  Missouri
1020 Lowry Street
Columbia, Missouri 65201
314-443-3165

Missouri Historical Society
P.O. Box 11940
St. Louis, Missouri 63112
314-746-4500

Montana Historical Society
225 North Roberts
Helena, Montana 59601
406-449-2694

Nebraska State Historical Society
1500 R Street
Lincoln, Nebraska 68508
402-471-3270

Nevada Historical Society
1650 North Virginia Street
Reno, Nevada 89503
702-784-6397

New Hampshire Historical
  Society
30 Park Street
Concord, New Hampshire 03301
603-225-3381

The New Jersey Historical
   Society
230 Broadway
Newark, New Jersey 07104
201-483-3939

Museum of New Mexico
History Bureau
Palace of Governors
North Side of Plaza
Santa Fe, New Mexico 87501
505-827-2921

State Records Center and
   Archives
404 Montezuma
Santa Fe, New Mexico 87503
505-827-2321

Historical Society of New Mexico
P.O. Box 5819
Santa Fe, New Mexico 87502

Division of History and
   Anthropology, New York
   State Museum
3099 Cultural Center
Empire State Plaza
Albany, New York 12230
518-474-1299

New York State Archives
Cultural Education Center
Empire State Plaza
Albany, New York 12230
518-474-1195

North Carolina Division of
   Archives and History
109 East Jones Street
Raleigh, North Carolina 27611
919-733-7305

State Historical Society of North
   Dakota
North Dakota Heritage Center
Bismarck, North Dakota 58505
701-224-2669

The Ohio Historical Society
1982 Velma Avenue
Columbus, Ohio 43211
614-297-2300

Oklahoma Historical Society
2100 North Lincoln Blvd.
Oklahoma City, Oklahoma 73105
405-521-2491

Oregon Historical Society
1230 S.W. Park Avenue
Portland, Oregon 97205
503-222-1741

Pennsylvania Historical and
   Museum Commission
William Penn Memorial Museum
3rd and North Streets
Harrisburg, Pennsylvania 17120
717-787-2891

Rhode Island Historical Society
52 Power Street
Providence, Rhode Island 02906
401-331-8575

South Carolina Department of
Archives and History
P.O. Box 22669
Columbia, South Carolina 29211
803-734-7914

South Dakota State Historical
  Society
Soldiers' & Sailors' Memorial
  Building
East Capitol Avenue
Pierre, South Dakota 57501
605-773-3615

South Dakota State Archives
Office of Cultural Preservation
State Library
Pierre, South Dakota 57501
605-224-3173

Tennessee Historical Commission
4721 Trousdale Drive
Nashville, Tennessee 37219
615-741-2371

Tennessee Historical Society
War Memorial Building
Nashville, Tennessee 37219
615-741-2660

Tennessee State Library and
  Archives
403 7th Avenue North
Nashville, Tennessee 37219
615-741-2764

Texas Historical Commission
1511 Colorado
Austin, Texas 78701
512-475-3092

Texas State Historical Association
SRH 2-306
University Station
Austin, Texas 78712
512-471-1525

Texas State Library and Archives
  Commission
1201 Brazos
Austin, Texas 78701
Mail: Box 12927 Capitol Station,
Austin, Texas 78711
512-475-2166

Utah State Historical Society
Crane Building, Suite 1000
307 West 2nd Street
Salt Lake City, Utah 84103
801-533-5755

Vermont Historical Society, Inc.
State Street
Montpelier, Vermont 05602
802-828-2291

Virginia Historical Society
428 North Blvd.
Richmond, Virginia 23221
804-358-4901

Virginia State Library
12th and Capitol
Richmond, Virginia 23219
804-768-8929

Washington State Historical
  Society
315 North Stadium Way
Tacoma, Washington 98403
206-593-2830

West Virginia Department of
  Culture and History: Archives
  and History Division
The Cultural Center
Capitol Complex
Charleston, West Virginia 25305
304-348-0230

State Historical Society of
   Wisconsin
816 State Street
Madison, Wisconsin 53706
608-262-3266

Wyoming State Archives,
   Museums and Historical
   Department
Barrett Building
Cheyenne, Wyoming 82002
307-777-7010

BIBLIOGRAPHICAL ESSAY

Historians who are conducting research on a farm will be able to place the history of a specific farm in perspective if they gain a broad understanding of the American past. In addition to the sources noted in the Suggested Readings section at the end of each chapter, the following books and articles will be useful for obtaining that knowledge in a variety of areas.

The most recent survey of the field is R. Douglas Hurt, *American Agriculture: A Brief History* (Ames: Iowa State University Press, 1994). This study provides an overview of the main economic, social, political, technological, and scientific developments in American agriculture from the colonial period to the present. Be sure to consult the suggested readings at the end of each chapter for more specialized sources. See also David B. Danbom, *Born in the Country: A History of Rural America* (Baltimore: Johns Hopkins University Press, 1995). Other studies that provide a working, but more limited summary, include William W. Cochrane, *The Development of American Agriculture: A Historical Analysis* 2d ed. (Minneapolis: University of Minnesota Press, 1993) and John T. Schlebecker, *Whereby We Thrive: A History of American Farming, 1607–1972* (Ames: Iowa State University Press, 1975). Schlebecker's study is not really a history of farming but it is a useful reference for changes in agricultural science and technology as well as land policy and marketing. For a topical approach to American agricultural history see Walter Ebeling, *The Fruited Plain: The Story of American Agriculture* (Berkeley: University of California Press, 1979).

Paul W. Gates provides an authoritative study of land policy in *History of Public Land Law Development* (Washington, D.C.: Government Printing Office, 1968). Anyone interested in this subject should also consult his collection of articles entitled *Land and Law in California: Essays on Land Policies* (Ames: Iowa State University Press, 1991). For a study that contends the land policy of the federal government has primarily served the wealthy, large-scale farmers and land speculators rather than small-scale farmers see John Opie, *The Law of the Land: Two Hundred Years of American Farmland Policy* (Lincoln: University of Nebraska Press, 1987). An excellent book on land policy during the frontier period is Malcolm J. Rohrbough, *The Land Office Business: The Settlement and Administration of American Public Lands, 1789–1837* (New York: Oxford University Press, 1968).

Historians who are interested in the agriculture of the northern United States, including the Midwest, should consult Percy Wells Bidwell and John I. Falconer, *History of Agriculture in the Northern United States, 1820–1860* (New York: Peter Smith, 1941). Essential studies include John C. Hudson, *Making the Corn Belt: A Geographical History of Middle-Western Agriculture* (Bloomington: Indiana University Press, 1994) and Allan G. Bogue, *From Prairie to Cornbelt: Farming on the Illinois and Iowa Prairies in the Nineteenth Century*, (1963; reprint, Ames: Iowa State University Press, 1994). Bogue provides a detailed study of pioneer farming, particularly in relation to production, marketing, and technological change.

Other important sources include: Douglas R. McMannis, *Colonial New England: A Historical Geography* (New York: Oxford University Press, 1975); Max George Schumacher, *The Northern Farmer and His Market During the Late Colonial Period* (New York: Arno Press, 1975); Lou Ferleger ed., *Agriculture and National Development: Views on the Nineteenth Century* (Ames: Iowa State University Press, 1990); and Clarence Danhof, *Change in Agriculture: The Northern United States, 1820–1870* (Cambridge: Harvard University Press, 1969). Danhof provides an excellent discussion on farm making, agricultural education, land titles, marketing, and technological and scientific change. For a sophisticated use of statistics as a research tool see Jeremy Atack and Fred Bateman, *To Their Own Soil: Agriculture in the Antebellum North* (Ames: Iowa State University Press, 1987). This study provides a broad-ranging analysis of economic and social changes.

For New England the historian should consult Howard S. Russell, *A Long, Deep Furrow: Three Centuries of Farming in New England* (Hanover, N.H.: University of New England Press, 1982); Harold Fisher Wilson, *The Hill-Country of Northern New England: Its Social and Economic History, 1790–1939* (New York: Columbia University Press, 1936); and John Donald Black, *The Rural Economy of New England* (Cambridge: Harvard University Press, 1950).

The historian who comes to southern agricultural history for the first time should begin with Charles Reagan Wilson and William

Ferris eds., *Encyclopedia of Southern Culture* (Chapel Hill: University of North Carolina Press, 1989) as well as the eleven volume series entitled *A History of the South* edited by Wendell Holmes Stephenson and E. Merton Coulter and published by the Louisiana University Press. These volumes cover the period from 1607–1980, and they are essential for any study of southern history. Matters of fact often can be resolved by relying on Lewis Cecil Gray's *History of Agriculture in the Southern United States to 1860*, 2 vols. (Gloucester, Mass.: Peter Smith, 1958). Gray takes a detailed, topical approach, beginning with the colonial period. Although he stresses commodity development, much like Bidwell and Falconer's study of the North, he also discusses foreign trade, credit, and social class.

Other essential studies of southern agriculture include Gilbert C. Fite, *Cotton Fields No More: Southern Agriculture, 1865–1980* (Lexington: University of Kentucky Press, 1984) and Pete Daniel, *Breaking the Land: The Transformation of Cotton, Tobacco, and Rice Cultures Since 1880* (Urbana: University of Illinois Press, 1985). Two useful studies of the sugar cane industry are: J. Carlyle Sitterson, *Sugar Country: The Cane Sugar Industry in the South, 1753–1950* (Lexington: University of Kentucky Press, 1953) and John Alfred Heitmann, *The Modernization of the Louisiana Sugar Industry, 1830–1910* (Baton Rouge: Louisiana State University Press, 1987).

The business aspects of cotton production, particularly regarding finance and marketing are solidly covered in Harold D. Woodman, *King Cotton & His Retainers* (Lexington: University of Kentucky Press, 1968). For two important studies of southern agriculture that emphasize economic and social history see Gavin Wright, *Old South, New South: Revolutions in the Southern Economy Since the Civil War* (New York: Basic Books, 1984) and Jack Temple Kirby, *Rural Worlds Lost: The American South, 1920–1960* (Baton Rogue: Louisiana State University Press, 1987).

A superb study of southern rural life is Edward L. Ayers, *The Promise of the New South: Life After Reconstruction* (New York: Oxford University Press, 1992). Pete Daniel cogently traces the major changes in southern rural life in "Transformation of the Rural South: 1930 to the Present," *Agricultural History* 55 (July 1981): 231–48 and "Going Among Strangers: Southern Reactions to World War II," *Journal of American History* 77 (December 1990): 886–911. For additional information about the agricultural experience of African American farmers see Loren Schweninger, *Black Property Owners in the South, 1790–1915* (Urbana: University of Illinois Press, 1990) and Theodore Rosengarten ed., *All God's Dangers: The Life of Nate Shaw* (New York: Knopf, 1974).

The best introduction to slavery is Peter Kolchin, *American Slavery, 1619–1877* (New York: Hill & Wang, 1993). See also Kenneth M. Stampp, *The Peculiar Institution: Slavery in the Antebellum South* (New York: Knopf, 1956). For studies based on class that offer important insights about agriculture and slavery see Eugene D. Genovese, *Roll Jordan Roll: The World the Slaves Made* (New York: Pantheon, 1974) and *The Political Economy of Slavery: Studies in the Economy and Society of the Slave South*, 2d ed. (Middleton, Conn.: Wesleyan University Press, 1989). James Oakes provides a contrasting, capitalist interpretation of slavery and southern agriculture in *The Ruling Race: A History of American Slaveholders* (New York: Knopf, 1982).

Examples of agricultural history on the state level include: Clarence Day, *Farming in Maine, 1860–1940* (Orono: University of Maine Press, 1963); R. Douglas Hurt, *Agriculture and Slavery in Missouri's Little Dixie* (Columbia: University of Missouri Press, 1992); Donald P. Jones, *The Economic and Social Transformation of Rural Rhode Island* (Boston: Northeastern University Press, 1992); James T. Lemon, *The Best Poor Man's Country: A Geographical Study of Early Southeastern Pennsylvania* (Baltimore: Johns Hopkins University Press, 1972); and Donald L. Winters, *Tennessee Farmers, Tennessee Farming: Antebellum Agriculture in the Upper South* (Knoxville: University of Tennessee Press, 1994).

Studies of agriculture on the Great Plains should begin with Walter Prescott Webb, *The Great Plains* (1931; reprint, Lincoln: University of Nebraska Press, 1981). Although this work is more than a half-century old, it remains a standard source for embarkation regarding matters such as settlement, water rights, and the cattle industry. The essential principle of environmental determinism that Webb stresses has been discounted, but much of this study remains useful.

Historians of the Great Plains should consider the Dust Bowl and the federal government's efforts to aid farmers in that region. This subject also offers an excellent opportunity to see how historians arrive at various interpretations. Three recent books provide different conclusions about the federal government's agricultural programs in the Dust Bowl. Donald Worster argues that capitalist exploitation of the land caused the Dust Bowl and that the federal government did not do enough to help farmers in the *Dust Bowl: The Southern Plains in the 1930s* (New York: Oxford University Press, 1979). Worster suggests that collectivist state planning was required to bring soil erosion under control. In contrast, Paul Bonnifield contends in *The Dust Bowl: Men, Dirt, and Depression* (Albuquerque: University of New Mexico Press, 1979) that the federal government interfered too much with the lives of Great Plains' farmers, and that it was responsible for economic misfortune on the Southern Great Plains. Another interpretation can be found in R. Douglas Hurt, *The Dust Bowl: An Agricultural and Social History* (Chicago: Nelson-Hall, 1981). This study argues that the federal government did as well as any one could expect under difficult environmental, political, and economic conditions. See also Pamela Riney-Kehrberg, *Rooted in Dust: Surviving Drought and Depression in Southwestern Kansas* (Lawrence: University Press of Kansas, 1994).

The best study of the livestock industry is Terry G. Jordan, *North American Cattle Ranching Frontiers* (Albuquerque: University of New Mexico Press, 1993). See also Jordan's *Trails to Texas: Southern Roots of Western Cattle Ranching* (Lincoln: University of Nebraska Press, 1981) in which he stresses British and southern antecedents rather than the Spanish heritage of the range cattle industry. Older, but still useful, studies include Ernest Staple Osgood's *Day of the Cattlemen* (1929; reprint, Chicago: University of Chicago Press, 1970). Lewis Atherton discusses the business aspects of cattle ranching in *The Cattle Kings* (Bloomington: Indiana University Press, 1961). For the twentieth century, see John T. Schlebecker, *Cattle Raising on the Plains, 1900–1961* (Lincoln: University of Nebraska Press, 1963). Schlebecker argues that cattlemen were not the epitome of independence, but rather a powerful, political interest group that sought government support with no strings attached. Four excellent studies of the marketing and meat packing aspects of the livestock industry are: Jimmy M. Skaggs, *Prime Cut: Livestock Raising in the United States, 1607–1982* (College Station: Texas A & M University Press, 1986); Margaret Walsh, *The Rise of the Midwestern Meat Packing Industry* (Lexington: University of Kentucky Press, 1982); Louise Carroll Wade, *Chicago's Pride: The Stock Yards, Packingtown, and Environs in the Nineteenth Century* (Urbana: University of Illinois Press, 1987); and J'Nell L. Pate, *Livestock Legacy: The Fort Worth Stockyards, 1887–1987* (College Station: Texas A & M University Press, 1988).

Essential books for understanding the Patrons of Husbandry are: Solon Justice Buck, *The Granger Movement* (1913; reprint, Lincoln: University of Nebraska Press, 1963); D. Sven Nordin, *Rich Harvest: A History of the Grange, 1867–1900* (Jackson: University of Mississippi Press, 1974); George H. Miller, *Railroads and the Granger Laws* (Madison: University of Wisconsin Press, 1971); and Thomas A. Wood, *Knights of the Plow: Oliver H. Kelley and the Origins of the Grange in Republican Ideology* (Ames: Iowa State University Press, 1991). Buck portrays the grange as a progressive, economic, and social organization with political power. Nordin, however, stresses the social and educational aspects of the grange, while Miller argues that the railroad magnates rather than the grange were responsible for the regulation of interstate commerce to ensure self-protection. Woods traces the origins of radicalism in the organization.

Any study of agrarian radicalism must include two works by Robert C. McMath Jr., *American Populism: A Social History, 1877–1898* (New York: Hill & Wang, 1993) and *Populist Vanguard: A History of the Southern Farmers' Alliance* (New York: W. W. Norton, 1975). See also John D. Hicks, *The Populist Revolt* (1931; reprint, Lincoln: University of Nebraska Press, 1961) for the economic troubles of western and southern farmers which views Populism as a progressive movement. In addition, consult Lawrence Goodwyn, *The Populist Moment: A Short History of the American Revolt in America* (New York: Oxford University Press, 1978). Goodwyn contends that the Populists emerged as a political force from the cooperative experience of the Farmers' Alliance and transformed into a mass political movement. He argues the Populists made valiant efforts to achieve democratic reform but failed. In contrast, Norman Pollack's works: *The Populist Response to Industrial America: Midwestern Populist Thought* (Cambridge: Harvard University Press, 1962); *The Humane Economy: Populism, Capitalism, and Democracy* (New Brunswick: Rutgers University Press, 1990); and *The Just Polity: Populism, Law and Human Welfare* (Urbana: University of Illinois Press, 1987) views the People's party as a progressive movement that would have altered the course of American history in a socialist direction. For Pollack, the Populists offered the last chance for the survival of radicalism in American economic, political, and social life. See also Gene Clanton, *Populism: The Humane Preference in America, 1890–1900* (New York: Twayne, 1991).

Studies of the Far West should include James R. Gibson, *Farming on the Frontier: The Agricultural Opening of the Oregon Country, 1786–1846* (Seattle: University of Washington Press, 1985); Lawrence H. Jelinek, *Harvest of Empire: A History of California Agriculture,* 2d ed. (San Francisco: Boyd and Fraser, 1982); Ellen Liebman, *California Farmland: A History of Large Agricultural Holdings* (Totowa, N.J.: Roman and Allenheld, 1983); and Michael P. Malone and Richard W. Etulian, *The American West: A Twentieth-Century History* (Lincoln: University of Nebraska Press, 1989).

The historian can pursue twentieth-century agricultural organizations in Theodore Saloutos and John D. Hicks, *Twentieth-Century Populism: Agricultural Dissent in the Middle West, 1900–1939* (Madison: University of Wisconsin Press, 1951), which provides an introduction to the major organizations and coalitions, such as the Farmers Union and Farm Bureau and the congressional farm bloc. Similarly, see also

Saloutos' study, *Farmer Movements in the South, 1865–1933* (Berkeley: University of California Press, 1960). Robert L. Morlan's *Political Prairie Fire: The NonPartisan League, 1915–1922* (1955; reprint, St. Paul: Minnesota Historical Society Press, 1985) emphasizes a specific and important aspect of the agrarian revolt. John Mark Hansen discusses the diminishing influence of farmers' organizations and the increasing power of agricultural lobbying groups based on commodities in *Gaining Access: Congress and the Farm Lobby, 1919–1981* (Chicago: University of Chicago Press, 1991).

Sources for twentieth-century agrarian radicalism should include Lowell K. Dyson, *Red Harvest: The Communist Party and American Farmers* (Lincoln: University of Nebraska Press, 1982) and John L. Shover, *Cornbelt Rebellion: The Farmers' Holiday Association* (Urbana: University of Illinois Press, 1965) for the Midwest. See also R. Douglas Hurt, "Farmers at the Barricades," *Timeline* 7 (June–July 1990): 18–33. Farm radicalism in the Upper South is the subject of Tracy Campbell, *The Politics of Despair: Power and Resistance in the Tobacco Wars* (Lexington: University of Kentucky Press, 1993); Christopher Waldrep, *Night Riders: Defending Community in the Black Patch, 1890–1915* (Durham: Duke University Press, 1993); and Suzanne Marshall, *Violence in the Black Patch of Kentucky and Tennessee* (Columbia: University of Missouri Press, 1994).

Joan M. Jensen provides an important analysis of the economic and social life of farm women in *Loosening the Bonds: Mid-Atlantic Farm Women, 1750–1850* (New Haven: Yale University Press, 1986). See also her study, *With these Hands: Women Working on the Land* (Old Westbury, N.Y.: Feminist Press, 1981) in which she discusses Indian, black, southern, and western women through agricultural stories told in their own words. Other studies that focus on the agricultural roles of women include: Sally McMurry, *Transforming Rural Life: Dairying Families and Agricultural Change, 1820–1885* (Baltimore: Johns Hopkins University Press, 1995); Mary Neth, *Preserving the Family Farm: Women, Community and the Foundations of Agribusiness in the Midwest, 1900–1940* (Baltimore: Johns Hopkins University Press, 1995); Deborah Fink, *Agrarian Women: Wives and Mothers in Rural Nebraska, 1880–1940* (Chapel Hill: University of North Carolina Press, 1992); Wava G. Haney and Jane B. Knowles, eds., *Women and Farming: Changing Roles, Changing Structures* (Boulder: Westview Press, 1988); Katherine Jellison, *Entitled to Power: Farm Women and Technology, 1913–1963* (Chapel Hill: North Carolina University Press, 1993); and Rachel Ann Rosenfeld, *Farm Women: Work, Farm, and Family in the United States* (Chapel Hill: University of North Carolina, 1985).

Any discussion about agricultural labor should draw upon Cletus E. Daniel, *Bitter Harvest: A History of California Farmworkers, 1870–1941* (Ithaca: Cornell University Press, 1981) as well as Craig Jenkins, *The Politics of Insurgency: The Farm Worker Movement in the 1960s* (New York: Columbia University Press, 1985). See also Carey Williams's poignant *Factories in the Fields: The Story of Migrant Farm Labor in California* (1935; reprint, Santa Barbara: Peregrine Smith, Inc., 1978).

Alan I Marcus provides an introduction to agricultural education and experiment station work in *Agricultural Science and the Quest for Legitimacy: Farmers, Agricultural Colleges, and Experiment Stations, 1870–1890* (Ames: Iowa State University Press, 1985). Marcus studies the agricultural experiment stations before the Hatch Act and analyzes the long and often bitter struggle between farmers and scientists for the creation and control of the agricultural experiment stations. Roy V. Scott provides a thorough discussion of agricultural extension in *The Reluctant Farmers: The Rise of Agricultural Extension to 1914* (Urbana: University of Illinois Press, 1970). Scott surveys the educational activities of farmer's institutes and the efforts of the agricultural colleges and railroads to improve agricultural knowledge. This study aptly covers the Smith-Lever Act, agricultural extension system, and the work of the county agents. A broad, commemorative overview of the extension service can be found in Wayne D. Rasmussen, *Taking the University to the People: Seventy-five Years of Cooperative Extension* (Ames: Iowa State University Press, 1989). Joel Schor surveys the agricultural education of one minority group in *Agriculture in the Black Land-Grant System to 1930* (Tallahassee, Fl.: Florida A & M University, 1982). Wayne E. Fuller provides an excellent discussion of rural education in *The Old Country School: The Story of Rural Education in the Middle West* (Chicago: University of Chicago Press, 1982); *One-Room Schools of the Middle West: An Illustrated History* (Lawrence: University Press of Kansas, 1994); and "Everybody's Business: The Midwestern One-Room School," *Timeline* 10 (September–October 1993): 32–47.

The origin and development of the United States Department of Agriculture is detailed in Gladys Baker et al., *Century of Service: The First Hundred Years of the United States Department of Agriculture* (Washington, D.C.: Department of Agriculture, 1963). A study designed for the nonprofessional historian is R. Douglas Hurt, *The Department of Agriculture* (New York: Chelsea House, 1989).

The farm historian with a basic familiarity with agricultural policy will be able to understand the relationship of the federal government to farming. Agricultural policy, however, can seem bewildering, technical, and difficult. Essential books that explain things clearly and simply are: Murray R. Benedict, *Farm Policies of the United States, 1790–1950: A Study of Their Origins and Development* (New York: Twentieth Century Fund, 1953); Willard W. Cochrane and Mary E. Ryan, *American Farm Policy, 1948–1973* (Minneapolis: University of Minnesota Press, 1976); and David Hamilton, *From New Day to New Deal: American Farm Policy from Hoover to Roosevelt, 1928–1933* (Chapel Hill: University of North Carolina Press, 1991). William P. Brown has written two important studies that show the importance of interest group politics to the making of agricultural policy, *Cultivating Congress: Constituents, Issues, and Interests in Agricultural Policy Making* (Lawrence: University Press of Kansas, 1995) and *Private Interests, Public Policy, and American Agriculture* (Lawrence: University Press of Kansas, 1988).

For the social and cultural aspects of the Progressive movement in American agriculture see William E. Bowers, *The Country Life Movement in America, 1900–1920* (Port Washington, N.Y.: Kennikat Press, 1974). David B. Danbom's *The Resisted Revolution: Urban America and the Industrialization of Agriculture, 1900–1930* (Ames: Iowa State University Press, 1979) provides a sharply contrasting view. Danbom argues that many of the Progressives were urban intellectuals who sought to improve agriculture through better organization and efficiency for the benefit of the city masses.

Any discussion of the New Deal should include an evaluation of the federal government's agricultural programs. Theodore Saloutos provides a good introduction to the diverse work of the Roosevelt administration in *The American Farmer and the New Deal* (Ames: Iowa State University Press, 1982). For study of an agricultural group that remained unaided by the New Deal see David E. Conrad, *The Forgotten Farmers: The Story of the Sharecroppers and the New Deal* (Urbana: University of Chicago Press, 1965) and Donald Grubbs, *Cry from the Cotton: The Southern Tenant Farmers Union and the New Deal* (Chapel Hill: North Carolina University Press, 1971).

For a useful overview of twentieth-century agriculture based on economic and political analysis, see Gilbert C. Fite, *American Farmers: The New Minority* (Bloomington: Indiana University Press, 1981). A more theoretical study is John L. Shover, *First Majority—Last Minority: The Transforming of Rural Life in America* (DeKalb: Northern Illinois University Press, 1976). This book provides excellent examples of social and technological change.

Historians who are studying children in American agriculture and rural life should consult, Elliot West, *Growing Up With the Country:*

Childhood on the Far Western Frontier (Albuquerque: University of New Mexico Press, 1989) and Elizabeth Hampston, *Settlers Children: Growing Up on the Great Plains* (Norman: University of Oklahoma Press, 1991).

These sources provide a place to begin. The bibliographies in each book, of course, offer suggestions for further learning. The historian who is writing the history of a farm should use these studies to help emphasize the manner in which technical, scientific, economic, political, and social change affected that farm as well as the manner in which it contributed to American agricultural history in general. The key is to stress cause, effect, and significance in order to understand not only historical developments but also the relationship of the farm to the past and present.

INDEX